Under Siege in Kuwait

Under Siege in Kuwait

A Survivor's Story

Jadranka Porter

Houghton Mifflin Company
Boston / 1991

For information about permission to reproduce
selections from this book, write to Permissions,
Houghton Mifflin Company, 2 Park Street,
Boston, Massachusetts 02108.

First American Edition

The right of Jadranka Porter to be identified as author
of this work has been asserted by her in accordance with
the Copyright, Designs and Patents Act of 1988.

CIP data is available.
ISBN 0-395-60580-6

First published in Great Britain in 1991 by Victor Gollancz Ltd.

Printed in the United States of America

AGM 10 9 8 7 6 5 4 3 2 1

Acknowledgements

This book is based on six volumes of notes I kept from the start of the invasion to my departure on March 10, 1991 and on letters written between August 29, 1990 and February 1991. I recorded the conversations and observations as they happened or within three days of their happening. I also recorded my reactions and feelings at the same time. The reflections came later.

I am indebted to a large number of people of many nationalities. They are too numerous to name in full, but they know who they are. I feel privileged to have known them and to have shared some of their experiences with them.

I would like to thank my parents and sister for their forbearance and understanding and Clem who was always in my thoughts. I would also like to thank Sandy and Eoin, Aziz, Ski and Ikuko, Vladimir and Hani for their kindness and support when things were toughest. I am grateful to my dear friends Susan and Nasser in England for keeping me in touch with life back home. My thanks to Joanna Goldsworthy for her patience and encouragement in the wiriting and to Alan without whom it would not have been possible.

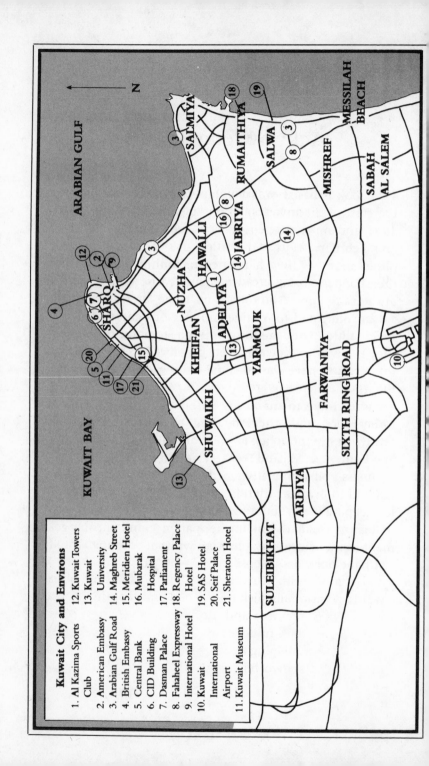

Kuwait City and Environs

1. Al Kazima Sports Club
2. American Embassy
3. Arabian Gulf Road
4. British Embassy
5. Central Bank
6. CID Building
7. Dasman Palace
8. Fahaheel Expressway
9. International Hotel
10. Kuwait International Airport
11. Kuwait Museum
12. Kuwait Towers
13. Kuwait University
14. Maghreb Street
15. Meridien Hotel
16. Mubarak Hospital
17. Parliament
18. Regency Palace Hotel
19. SAS Hotel
20. Seif Palace
21. Sheraton Hotel

Preface

The Kuwait of pre-war days was one of the most prosperous and modern states in the world with a population of almost two million people, more than half of whom were expatriates of many nationalities. From its five-star hotels to its super highways, from its towering office blocks to its smart shopping arcades, from its swish limousines to its chic beach resorts and leisure centres, it reeked of wealth.

Many expatriates enjoyed lives of an affluence and style hardly conceivable in their homelands. As a result, though Kuwait was an area in which upheaval often threatened, they were content to turn a blind eye and ignore what was no business of theirs. It was not always easy to look the other way. But somehow they managed it. Even when Iraq's war with Iran drew close to the city of Basra up the Gulf, and gunfire rattled their seafront windows, they put it down to distant thunder and gave their plastic bins of fermenting grape juice another stir.

In those days, Iraq and Kuwait were allies and, although Saddam Hussein was often on the run from the Iranians, few had any real doubt he would ultimately see off 'the mullahs'. Those rare Western expatriates who had contact with Kuwaitis outside their luxury offices would occasionally pick up the odd hint that things were not all they seemed; and, despite their alliance, it was known there was no love lost between Iraq and Kuwait.

Kuwait was helping to bankroll Iraq's war efforts to the tune of nearly two billion dollars a year. It was under some pressure to do so. Iraq had miscalculated in forecasting an easy victory against Iran, and now presented itself as the region's defender against the fundamentalist fanatics in Tehran. But Kuwait also paid up to keep Iraq's covetous eyes off its territory, to which Baghdad had long staked a claim.

Even as the Iran–Iraq war went on there were periodic rumblings over these and other problems between the two countries, and Iraqi troops were at one time rumoured to have landed on the islands of Bubiyan and Warba, which were later to be seized in August 1990. There had also been a number of terrorist bombings in Kuwait during the 1980s and among those arrested were some who were suspected of having enjoyed safe haven in Baghdad.

It was also clear that all was not well within Kuwait. There was an assassination attempt on the Amir in 1985 and there had been a suicide bombing attack against the American Embassy in 1983. There was also the scandal surrounding the collapse of the reserve stock exchange which was effectively being used as a giant gambling casino. When the bubble burst in 1982, the combined losses amounted to a staggering $92 billion.

The government, steeped in paternalism and embarrassed by the involvement of some in high places, spent the 1980s trying to sort out the economic mess. It would have toppled any genuinely elected government. As it was, the Amir disbanded the National Assembly in 1986. At the time the suspension only really caused a stir among the politicians themselves but, in the longer term, it swelled the ranks of the government's critics and increased pressure for a genuinely democratic government. The opposition's discontent mounted as the wave of revolutions swept across Eastern Europe. When Kuwaitis took to the streets to demonstrate in late 1989, the government sent in police with tear gas, dogs and watercannon to disperse them and there were a number of arrests. But the protests did result in a National Council being set up by the government to pave the way for the reinstatement of the National Assembly. It never did. It met for the first time in June, less than two months before the Iraqi invasion.

Kuwait was always a hotbed of gossip and rumour, because facts were hard to come by. They circulated freely on the expatriate cocktail and diplomatic circuit though expatriates were more concerned with dining out on their latest snippets of gossip than with sorting the truth from the fiction.

While the United States, Britain and the rest of the Western world were feeling the pinch from high oil prices and job losses, the expatriates were enjoying the fruits of the very boom which was causing the discomfort at home. And though by 1990 the oil boom was over – and expatriates had been eased out as a result – for those who stayed, the good life was still in evidence and being enjoyed to the full.

When the Iraqis invaded on August 2, I had lived and worked for five years in Kuwait as a reporter for the *Arab Times*, an English language daily newspaper belonging to the Al Seyassah group. Before that, I had spent seven years on a paper in Bahrain. Being a journalist in the Gulf was neither as materially rewarding nor as professionally satisfying as being a Western expatriate in business or commerce. Compared to bankers, construction workers, engineers, architects and consultants, we were paid a pittance. But the main problem was gathering information in a country in which rumour flourished and people were deeply suspicious and afraid of having their views and activities made public.

The Kuwaiti government was congenitally secretive.

7

Even before 1986, when censors were officially introduced in newspaper offices, unspecified constraints were in force. Editors were expected to know the guidelines and avoid issues and areas regarded as sensitive. The possibilities of what might offend were so wide-ranging and changing, many played safe in the extreme. It resulted in the blandest of news coverage. The more shrewd and conscientious learned how to write around sensitive subjects by using a kind of code language and burying a point deep down the story.

Unlike many expatriates, and even diplomats, my job brought me into contact with a wide cross-section of people of all nationalities, from both East and West, Asia, Europe and the American continent. I regularly did the diplomatic cocktail circuit, and also met a large number and variety of visiting businessmen, politicians and senior military people who popped in and out at regular intervals because of Kuwait's commercial importance, and because of its strategic position in the Gulf. With access to this sort of information, I felt I had my ear close to the ground.

As it turned out, when the Iraqis invaded I was no better prepared than any other expatriate. But then neither were the governments of the United States, Britain, France, or indeed the rest of the world.

Under Siege in Kuwait

I

They picked us up, the two Kuwaitis, from the round-about in front of the Sheraton Hotel near the centre of the city.

It was February 26, 1991, and liberation day was only a few hours old. Kuwait City was empty apart from small groups who had ventured out, not quite sure if it was too early to celebrate. Only as we rounded the bend from Fahad Al Salem Street near the Meridien Hotel was it clear we were on a hunting trip.

The Iraqi soldier was about two hundred metres ahead on the left. He was trudging along, his head down and his back to us. He had a kalashnikov rifle slung over his right shoulder. The two Kuwaitis began talking excitedly and pointing at him. Talal, who was driving the Chevrolet, accelerated fast past the soldier and, about 50 metres on, did a U-turn and slowed down. As we passed by, our eyes were locked on his every movement. He looked about fifty years old. He was dressed in brown-green camouflage battle fatigues. His face looked lined and tired and as we passed he did not even glance up.

Talal pulled up about 100 metres down the road. He and his friend grabbed rifles from somewhere between the front seat and the floor. Talal had a Belgian assault rifle FAL 7.62 Nato, which was standard Kuwait Army issue. His friend had an MP5 Hackler Khoch 9m sub-machine-gun. He also had a revolver stuck in the waist-band of his trousers. They jumped out of the car and I watched them take up firing positions. Talal crouched

11

behind an empty barrel of the kind the Iraqis had used for roadblocks; his friend stood beside the wall of a parking lot. Karl, my American neighbour, was on the back seat with me. I knew he was carrying a revolver and he pulled it out from his coat pocket. He threw open the back door and rolled on to the street, before ending up crouched in front of the bonnet.

I was now on my own.

Everything seemed to happen at once. Talal shouted something at the soldier. The soldier stopped and half-turned. He was directly in my line of sight. Just before the first shot, I went down. It sounded so loud I think it must have come from the soldier. I was flat on the seat. My heart was racing and I was silently cursing. Then there were more shots.

For a moment I thought: 'Bloody hell, I am going to die.' I was angry. I thought to myself: 'This is stupid. I went through all the shit over seven months and now I'm going to get killed.'

I felt my nails dig into the velvet covers. It seemed like ages, but it must have been only a few seconds. Then nothing.

I was afraid to lift my head. Then I saw Karl through the open door moving on his haunches towards me. He was still pointing his revolver in the direction of the Iraqi soldier. I lifted my head and peered through the back window. The Kuwaitis were running in the direction the soldier had last been seen, but he had disappeared, probably into one of the alleys and buildings close by. Like the rest of the Iraqi garrison in Kuwait City he had fled as suddenly as he had appeared.

I had awoken that morning to the sound of gunfire. There had been many such mornings over the past six months and twenty-four days. The difference this time was that these were the parting shots of a retreating army.

II

It was a different kind of gunfire which half-woke me at about 5.30 a.m. on Thursday August 2, 1990. It did not fully register at the time and sounded something like thunder in the distance. I turned over and went back to sleep. Clem, who is normally an early riser, seemed not to notice. He had just got back from a vacation in the United States and was still recovering from jetlag.

It must have been fifteen minutes later when the phone rang. I thought it was a call from his relatives and grumbled into the pillow. Clem's side of the conversation was brief. He just said 'Hello' and 'OK', and replaced the hand-set.

It was one of his workmates, another American training officer at the Kuwait Ministry of Defence. Iraq had attacked Kuwait.

'*What?*'

'All Americans are being told to stay indoors until further notice,' said Clem.

I was now wide awake and when a gun again rumbled, this time there was no mistaking it. Clem and I looked at each other in disbelief. I reached for the radio, permanently tuned to the BBC. It was true. The invasion was at that moment being confirmed but, by the sound of the gunfire, we knew the Iraqis must already be close to the city.

This was war and we were suddenly in the middle of it. I couldn't believe it. A whole stream of thoughts flooded in. Where are they? How close? There was no

13

shooting outside, but I could still hear the guns. Clem didn't say anything. He seemed lost in his own thoughts. Apart from anything else, our weekend was ruined.

Only yesterday we had been planning our first free day together for more than a month. Since we had met the year before, our lives had been a series of separations interspersed with reunions as Clem and I pursued the demands of our jobs. But when we were not abroad or working we did the same kind of things as other Western expatriates living in Kuwait. Weekends were precious.

I had lived with Clem for eight months. We met at a dance in the Regency Palace Hotel in May 1989. He was a military adviser at the Ministry of Defence in Kuwait and, unusual among Americans there, he was also black. At fifty-seven this was possibly his last job before retirement. Not so me. Clem and I were in many ways very different. I was born in Yugoslavia and was British by marriage. I was seventeen years younger and since my divorce, more than ten years before, I had lived on my own – until I met Clem. I had worked all that time in the Gulf, the last five years in Kuwait as a journalist on the *Arab Times*. Unlike Clem, retirement was a long way off, and I was deeply into my career. I was the one whose travels overseas were most responsible for our periods of separation. There were other differences between us. I was a free agent. I had one marriage behind me, Clem had several. I had no children. Clem had six, four of whom he was still supporting. He could afford it because he was one of the better-paid expatriates in the country.

Like most expatriates enjoying the good life we were content to live from day to day. Any plans we might have had for the future were only discussed in the vaguest terms, and mostly we were caught up in the general tide of complacency that pervaded the expatriate community and even the Kuwaitis themselves.

That August morning, the gunfire shook us into a reality we had hardly experienced in all our time in Kuwait. But it took some time to register. Our apartment in Salwa overlooked the intersection near the Messilah Beach Hotel. We were about 25 kilometres south of Kuwait City and from our balcony we could just glimpse the Gulf. It was only about 100 metres away but a row of villas partly obscured the view. Now, as we jumped out of bed and dashed to the living-room window, there was nothing to suggest that this was anything but an ordinary Thursday morning. Everything looked normal and strangely peaceful. The sound of guns had stopped, the sun was up, the trees shading the chalets round the hotel were waving gently and the sea was glittering. There were only a few cars on the road but this was not unusual for the early hour.

Clem picked up the phone and called the American Embassy. They told him they were busy and hung up. It was very frustrating. We knew there was danger approaching but we did not know from which direction or when it would reach us. Our anxiety mounted by the minute – we just didn't know what to do.

It was a relief when the phone rang again and I heard the voice of John Roberts who worked in London for an oil magazine. 'I haven't slept the whole night,' he told me. 'Iraq has attacked and the Americans are calling it a major offensive.' He seemed to know more than we did. Only the day before he had called, asking me about reported Iraqi penetration into Kuwait. I had been unable to confirm it.

This was not unusual. Kuwait was never an easy place to gather information. I had been trying for days to keep abreast of developments in the dispute between Kuwait and Iraq. The row was over a long list of Iraqi demands. They were accusing Kuwait of depressing the oil market

15

by overproduction. They also wanted Kuwait to forgo $14 billion it had loaned them for their war with Iran. There were territorial claims as well for two Kuwaiti offshore islands, Warba and Bubiyan. Each day Baghdad seemed to be making new demands. Kuwait was taking more than its share of oil from the Rumailah field which straddles the border. None of the claims was new but this was the first time they had all come at the same time.

Iraq was in bad shape after its war with Iran and was desperately short of money. To any close watcher of the situation, which I was, it seemed as though Iraq was looking for a pretext for war. Yet nobody, including me, really thought it would happen. When we had gone to bed the night before, the talks in Jeddah were deadlocked but were set to resume in Baghdad. It looked like becoming one of those typically protracted Arab disputes. So much for inside knowledge.

An hour after John rang we saw the first tanks rolling past the intersection near the hotel only 50 metres away. They were heading towards the city. I counted dozens of them. They were followed by scores of trucks carrying troops in combat gear, with water and gasoline tankers coming up behind. Yet, even then, I was not sure they were Iraqis. There was no way of identifying them and they could have been Kuwaiti troops moving up to the front. I rushed up to the roof with my camera. I had never seen anything like it.

The intersection was clogged with tanks and trucks and troop carriers and there were civilian cars weaving their way in and out and causing the most gigantic traffic jam. My German neighbour was trying to identify them through binoculars. The tanks were flying red flags. And then the helicopters arrived. They came roaring over our heads in groups of three and four and five. They made a tremendous racket and were like swarms of hornets. I think it was then that I realised these *had* to be the Iraqis, but I was too amazed by the spectacle to feel any apprehension. If anything, I felt a sense of exhilaration. I watched soldiers getting on and off their trucks for a breather and taking swigs of water from their canteens. The heat from the sun was fierce by this time and they were in full battle fatigues. Some were looking around and when they looked in my direction I realised they could see my head and shoulders above the parapet of the roof. I rushed downstairs to join Clem in the flat. From the window I saw soldiers taking up positions in the streets.

Clem had tried to stop me going out on the roof. He felt the danger more acutely, I think. He had spent a year in Vietnam with the US Air Force in the late 1960s and had seen the battle for Da Nang. He had not talked about it much but I sensed it had left a deep impression on him. Now he was calm but pensive and said hardly anything, while I rushed from window to window, feeling a mixture of rising fear and excitement — just living the moment.

When the phone rang it was an Arab friend to tell us Kuwait Radio was still on the air and announcing repeatedly: 'The day of sacrifice has come,' and calling on everyone to rise up against the invaders.

I thought: 'Some hope!' For the first time what was happening began to sink in. I was watching this enormous army, and the idea that anyone could rise against it seemed ridiculous. We had no guns and my main thought was: 'How are we going to save ourselves?'

We weren't the only ones.

The phone began ringing from all parts of the city. Everyone, all my friends, were in a panic. They wanted to know what we were going to do and what they should do. Some were already thinking of ways to escape. Others told me what was happening where they lived as the Iraqi troops fanned out over the city.

One of those close to the action was Chris Monk, a computer specialist at the Kuwait investment bank, who lived with his wife Kate on the eighth floor of an apartment block overlooking the Dasman Palace, which was the home of the Amir. Over the phone Chris gave me a running commentary of the battle taking place at the palace. He could hardly conceal his excitement. Two stray bullets had just come through the window and landed in his kitchen.

The battle had begun at 5.30 a.m., just about the time I rolled over in my sleep. The Iraqis had come with tanks, armoured personnel carriers and helicopters to attack the palace. Since then it had been under almost constant fire. What neither Chris nor I knew then was that most of the royal family had fled the palace soon after the Iraqis crossed the border, and were now safe in Riyadh. It was being defended by the only leading member of the family who remained. When Iraqi troops began to storm it, guns firing, Sheikh Fahd, the Amir's younger brother, stood on the palace steps, firing back with automatic rifles. Before he fell dead he is believed to have killed thirteen of the Iraqis. Sheikh Fahd had a reputation as a fiery, impulsive man and looked a formidable figure with his thick black beard and piercing eyes. In the late 1960s, much to the displeasure of the Amir, he had gone to fight with the Palestinians in Lebanon. To curb his impetuosity, on his return he was given the relatively minor job of head of the Kuwaiti Olympic Committee. Because he saw no future in government he was determined to make a name for himself on the world sports scene and was already head of the Asian Olympic Movement. He was headed for international Olympic honours when he was cut down on the steps of the palace.

The battle was still raging as Chris spoke. He described seeing Iraqi soldiers taking three civilians from the palace with their hands tied behind their backs and watched them escorted to a command post close to the British Embassy 200 metres away. He also saw three dead bodies lying on the beach. They were in uniform but he couldn't tell whether they were Iraqis or Kuwaitis. People were being rounded up and taken on to the beach before being moved. Chris didn't know where. It was while Kate was on the phone that I heard a deafening explosion over the line. She said: 'I must go,' and rang off. That was the last time I was to speak to her in Kuwait. The sudden violence was in as sharp contrast to Kate's life as it was to ours. She was an entomologist who spent much of her time on trips to Africa studying insect life. She was a gentle, scholarly type utterly absorbed in her work. Nothing could have been more foreign to her than guns going off within yards of her home.

Though second-hand, the Monks' account of the fighting around the palace was my first contact with the violence taking place outside. Chris had sounded almost elated telling me what was happening. It was as if he were in a privileged position and that he was claiming the first bullets through his window as trophies. I almost envied him. But I was also thrown off balance by the knowledge that it was happening at all. I had never believed that these two Arab states would ever actually come to blows.

As the calls came in, I related them to Clem. I was becoming increasingly agitated but he seemed able to stay detached. He just listened and nodded and got on with more practical things. He prepared lunch. I can't for the life of me remember what we ate.

As the day wore on, the details were being filled in. The Turkish counsellor Gursel Demirok described how

2,500 Iraqi commandos came in on the first wave before dawn to begin the attack on the Dasman Palace. There were also battles at the Seif Palace on the seafront, which was the Amir's workplace. Iraqi troops were now raiding the gold souk. They were entering the maze of little jewellery shops and stripping them bare. The banks were emptied of their gold bullion. When they could not get hold of the safe combinations, the troops planted charges and blew them apart. People tried to get at their money, but the cash machines were switched off at breakfast-time and the banks never opened. At the time it seemed the least of our worries, even though we had $30,000 deposited in two of them.

We were more concerned about food. We had our usual three- or four-day supply and were reasonably stocked up. In the panic outside, huge crowds descended on the supermarkets, emptying their shelves of anything from catfood to toilet paper. The first things to go were canned goods, as if people were stocking up for a long haul. The petrol stations were also struggling to cope, with long lines of cars asking to be filled up. The drivers were trying to ensure themselves a means of escape.

The first hint of trouble to come came in a call from Zeinab, an Indian friend, married to a Kuwaiti shipper. Her teenage son had been filming an Iraqi troop concentration near their home in Suleibikhat, a northern suburb. The driver of a passing Iraqi tank stopped, climbed down, and snatched the camera away. He threw it on the ground, drew his pistol and deliberately fired a bullet straight into it. He then told the terrified youth: 'You're lucky it was me who caught you, or it would have been you lying on the ground now.' It struck me it could have been me, too. Only hours before, the Iraqi soldiers had looked up and seen me on the rooftop with my camera.

I told her and she warned me: 'For goodness sake, don't do that again, you could get yourself killed.'

It was a relief therefore when someone called to say that though the Iraqis were stopping people to check identity cards and frisking people for arms, they were behaving courteously, especially towards women. But hard on the heels of that initial, optimistic report, came the first news of atrocities. A British Airways stewardess was reportedly raped in her room at the SAS Hotel only a few kilometres down the coast from where I lived. In a house close by, a German woman was raped when Iraqi soldiers came in their first sweep of the area. They were entering houses at random. Some of them were running amok, manhandling the occupants, looting whatever caught their eye. Women were their favourite target and there were countless reports of women, particularly Indians and Filipinos, being molested. I knew that if it could happen to them, it could happen to me, and my early euphoria began to evaporate fast.

It was about now that it occurred to us that perhaps we should be trying to escape. Although some of my friends raised the subject on the phone, I hadn't really thought seriously about it. Then about five in the after-noon we had a call telling us the first Westerners had fled. Some Americans from the oil town of Ahmedi, about 30 kilometres south of us, had managed to drive the 50 kilometres to the Saudi border. Apart from their proximity to Saudi Arabia, it was likely that the Iraqis had not yet reached the oil town. Judging from the confusion of the reports of what was going on in Kuwait City, an escape was probably quite easy for the Americans if they kept their heads down.

I tried to call a friend in Ahmedi to find out what was happening down there, but the lines were down. I was able to get the director of Shuaiba Port at his home close by and he told me he was at that moment trying to decide whether to make a dash for the border with his wife and son. His indecision was caused by the news that the border crossing was besieged by a queue of cars several kilometres long and nobody knew how close the Iraqis had moved towards it.

They were closer than we thought. Two Yugoslavs with two Italians and an Arab had set out for the border in the early hours of the invasion and had passed the Kuwaiti border-post when they saw a long queue of American and Kuwaiti cars in no man's land. Rather than wait in the queue, they decided to rest at the seaside resort of Khairan, a few kilometres back inside Kuwait. It was their undoing. Iraqi troops overtook them and they were arrested.

By the evening of that first day Clem was bemoaning what he thought was a missed chance. He had a powerful Fifth Avenue limousine and he said: 'We should have got into the car as soon as we had that first phone call at 5.30 this morning. We could have been at the border in an hour, before the Iraqis even got here.' This thought was to dog him for the next six weeks. By now it seemed too late. The troops had already set up roadblocks and checkpoints, including one at the intersection outside the flat. The whole city appeared to be sealed off. On TV we saw the Iraqi people marching through the streets of Baghdad, proclaiming Kuwait and Iraq as one nation. 'Long live the Kuwaiti revolution,' they chanted.

The realisation that we were now captives began to dawn on us.

I suddenly thought of my parents. They would be worried sick. They live in Belgrade and I had last talked to them three weeks before, after returning from visiting my sister in Turin. They are very dear to me and I now tried to get through to them. The lines were still up but it was impossible to get a connection to Yugoslavia. I did manage to reach John Roberts in London and passed on what information I had. Talking to someone outside lifted a great weight from my mind.

Alan Brown, my former editor at the *Arab Times*, called from England, promising to phone again on Friday morning. The call never came. By Thursday night all international lines were cut and many people would have to wait months before they could again speak to their loved ones back home.

III

I have long had the habit of assessing my entire life in the few minutes after opening my eyes in the morning, as if to decide whether the day will be worth living. I had had some miserable mornings in the past, usually when things had happened to shatter my sense of security. I remember how depressed I was when I heard, when I lived in Bahrain, that the secret police were making inquiries about me after I had written what I thought was a fairly innocent article about a Muslim Shia village. Only months before the invasion I had many moments of anguish about articles I had sent to London on Kuwait's pro-democracy movement. The Kuwaiti government was deporting journalists for writing such stories. I felt these worries much more sharply first thing in the morning.

On the second day of the invasion, the moment I awoke, the drama of the day before hit me with a sudden force. My exhilaration had gone. Instead, I felt menaced. And more drama was on the way. Not only did I have soldiers on my doorstep early in the morning but, in the stream of bad news that followed, we learnt that, yes, we were a target: the Iraqis were picking up the Britons and Americans.

The first thing I saw from what was now my watchpost by the living-room window were the Iraqis. There were some half a dozen of them less than 50 metres away. They were jumping over the wall of a villa which had been left unfinished by the builders. It was the closest I had been to them and I was afraid their next stop might

24

be our apartment building. I could see the soldiers but they could not see me behind the dark, reflective glass of our windows. The Egyptian caretaker of the building site was fussing around the soldiers, running to and fro at their bidding. When I saw them take off their shirts and wash, three at a time, from the water tanks used by the building workers, I relaxed a bit. Suddenly, two of them began to walk over the sandpatch towards our building. This was it, I thought. I froze. Just then, our Palestinian neighbours downstairs ran out to meet them. I breathed with relief. All the Iraqis wanted was food and water.

Later, one of our neighbours told me: 'We gave them what they asked for, but the danger is that if you give it to one, more will keep coming.' He advised us to draw the curtains at night and switch off the lights.

This incident reinforced our fear that, as Westerners, Clem and I were more trapped than others. We were waiting for instructions from our embassies but we either couldn't get through or they were too busy to talk to us. The shooting had stopped but none of our Western friends was venturing out. I suppose we all felt more conspicuous and, anyway, the American and British governments had been quick to line up to denounce Saddam Hussein and condemn the invasion. With our governments taking the leading role and likely to lead any retaliatory strike, Clem and I felt extremely vulnerable. Our state of mind wasn't improved by the ugly rumours that kept coming in via the telephone. At the SAS and Regency Palace Hotels, only a short distance away, we heard that fifty people had been killed and two hundred Kuwaitis shot dead at the Kuwait Oil Company building in Ahmedi. An Indian colleague at the *Arab Times* spoke of hundreds of people being rounded up for breaking the first curfew. A Filipino was also shot resisting arrest. Kuwait Radio was announcing that all contact had been lost with the outside world and was appealing for help. I switched on the TV but it had stopped broadcasting. I was anxious not to miss anything of what was going on, and was constantly on the phone, partly to get an idea of our own predicament and partly to gather information which I hoped somehow to pass on to London.

Every now and again the gunfire would start up again and then subside. Battles were still going on, both around the Bayan Palace where the government normally met and the Sha'ab Palace where the Prime Minister lived. Then the troops returned. About lunchtime we saw large numbers arrive in trucks and take over the Messilah Beach Hotel. Clem immediately sprang into action. He picked up the phone and called a colleague who was staying in the hotel and got through without trouble. He told Clem they had been ordered to stay in their rooms.

Each new phone call seemed to bring fresh news of violence. Groups of young Kuwaitis demonstrating in Hawalli, the main Palestinian area of the city, had been shot at by Iraqis from a Mercedes carrying Kuwaiti number plates. When the Iraqis themselves had come under fire, they fled. All signs of organised life seemed to be breaking down and, with the buildup of troops nearby, I began to feel as if a noose was tightening around us.

The anxiety was getting the better of me. I was convinced the Iraqis were going to come for us. Clem's job at the Defence Ministry seemed to make him a prime target for arrest and interrogation, though I thought the fact that he was black might work in his favour. (The Arabs have a contradictory attitude towards race. They can be quite callous in their treatment of Indians, and even to Arabs of darker skin, but given a straight choice in a crisis like this, I thought they might be sympathetic to a black man, especially an American.)

Later that day came the news I feared most. Demirok,

the Turkish Counsellor, rang to say that Iraqi soldiers had begun picking up American and British nationals. This seemed to confirm that we had been right to stay indoors. But the news came just at the wrong moment because, shortly afterwards, Nirmala, an Indo-Dutch colleague from the *Arab Times*, rang to advise me to get down to the newspaper's office to pick up my passport. I didn't know what to do. Clem didn't want me to go out. But under the circumstances I felt stateless without my British passport. I had my Yugoslav one but that was out of date. Nirmala had said I ought to act quickly. The office might not be open for much longer.

Passports were traditionally held by employers as an insurance against expatriates leaving the country without paying their debts. I decided to go to collect it. I dressed carefully, covering my hair with a scarf. To avoid attracting attention I didn't put on any make-up. I took my Yugoslav passport, so that I had some identification in case I was stopped, but I left behind my identity card showing I was a British journalist. Clem urged me to be careful and we said goodbye.

It was hot outside in the afternoon sun and I squinted in the brightness. I got in my car and set off, clutching the steering wheel tightly and looking straight ahead. There seemed to be soldiers and army vehicles everywhere but I thought if I did not look at them they would not see me. I noticed the damage done to the road surface by the tanks' tracks, but was so scared I didn't connect it with the buzzing noise the car made as it went over them. I was afraid something was wrong with the car and that I might have to stop. In twenty minutes I was at the newspaper.

Inside the building the Egyptian aide to the publisher was holding forth to a group of other Arabs on the state of the nation. He broke off and told someone to get my

27

passport. Within minutes, I was back in the car and on my way home. I had gone about halfway when I suddenly thought: 'We need food,' and headed for the Sultan Centre in Salwa, a supermarket not too far from my home.

Outside, a tall distinguished-looking man of about fifty was supervising a queue of shoppers anxious to get in. I recognised him as Dr Abdul Aziz Sultan. His family owned a chain of Sultan stores throughout the city and the year before, I had interviewed him when he became chairman of the Gulf Bank. I tried to sound casual, which was more than I felt. 'Changed jobs?' I smiled as I went in. I was not sure whether he recognised me, but he nodded and smiled back.

Inside, the shelves were emptying fast. Bread was being rationed to one loaf per person. I grabbed mine and some vegetables, cheese and packets of salami. The store had run out of milk so I got buttermilk as a substitute. All around me other people were cramming their baskets with whatever they could find. There was an odd spirit of community among the shoppers. Although it was terribly crowded and people were grabbing whatever they could lay their hands on, everyone was polite and smiled at each other.

On the way home I saw trucks full of soldiers ahead of me and was tempted to make for the first exit road to avoid them. Only the presence of other cars on the road made me drive on. I dreaded seeing uniforms, but nobody seemed to be interested in me. Groups of soldiers were going about their business, no one was being stopped, but I still felt that any time they might rush in the road and flag me down. When I got home I could see Clem was relieved to see me. I described my journey to him, kilometre by kilometre, excited that I had made the trip, though, now I was home, the experience made me feel no more confident.

Later that afternoon the Iraqis began broadcasting on Kuwait TV for the first time, declaring: 'The Al Sabah rule is over.' They were trying to show that a popular Kuwaiti uprising, in support of the invading Iraqis, had succeeded, but we knew this was a lie. There had been a lot of confusion but it had all been caused by the Iraqis. There had been no uprising and when I spoke to the director of Shuaiba Port I asked him if any Kuwaiti opposition leaders had been supporting the Iraqis. He told me: 'Definitely not.' His brother was one of the opposition leaders and they had been in close touch. When the Iraqis announced the formation of an interim government, they said it was made up of Kuwaitis but conspicuously did not name them, and when the government was eventually named, nobody had ever heard of its members. Later I learnt that the Iraqis did try to recruit some prominent Kuwaitis among those who had stayed behind and those who were overseas, but were given short-shrift. So they rounded up any Kuwaitis they could find to give the new government some semblance of credibility. They managed to find a Kuwaiti accountant with an Iraqi mother and appointed him head of government. There was a story that a member of the coastguard had been appointed to the cabinet. Most of them were coerced. They were put in military uniform and then on television. They were not recognised by the vast mass of Kuwaitis, who laughed at such inept tactics. Soon the Iraqis realised they were not serving their purpose and the members of the so-called government suddenly disappeared. No one seemed to know what became of them.

Late that second night Hetti Liberdim called from the International Hotel about 20 kilometres from us north up the coast road. Hetti was a Dutch radio journalist who had arrived only a week before the invasion. She had been assigned to send voice reports back to Holland on the developing dispute between Iraq and Kuwait. She was based in Cyprus and we were to have met but the invasion intervened. Now she told me that the guests at the hotel had been told by the Austrian manager, Herman Simon, to keep their heads down. They were instructed to sleep in the ground-floor rooms, or in the ballroom which had been used for some of Kuwait's grandest functions.

The hotel was just across from the American Embassy which was the best-protected building in the city. It still had concrete barriers in front of it as a precaution against a repeat of a suicide attack in 1983 by the driver of a truck filled with explosives. The International Hotel was rumoured to be a command centre for the Iraqi Army in Kuwait, which meant that their generals were only a stone's throw away from the American ambassador's office. There were a number of Americans among the guests in the hotel. Later some of them would seek refuge in their embassy but for now they were told to pack their bags and be ready for a possible evacuation. The manager had arranged buses for their departure and had told them: 'Be ready for any eventuality.'

The evacuation never took place. Within a few days, the Iraqis began a sweep of the hotels, rounding up all Western visitors.

IV

The Iraqi soldiers came again on Saturday. There were only two of them this time and they walked through our gate and knocked on our front door. I watched them approach. They were young, in their late teens, and wearing their shabby khaki uniforms and carrying rifles. Since I had seen the others washing across the road, the whole fact of their presence had unnerved me. It was the idea that at some time I might come face to face with one. Then what? Now they were downstairs. I feared the worst. Clem and I didn't dare move. Neither did our downstairs neighbours, who didn't answer the door. I watched from a window and after a minute or two I saw them go and join a group of others across the street. One of them began to try out an old skateboard. He was not very good at it and kept losing his balance. The other soldiers laughed, he laughed, and for a moment they looked like a bunch of schoolboys at play. They were not much older and I found it hard to believe that they could be responsible for any of the brutality we'd heard about.

The first confirmation that the Iraqis had begun taking hostages came with a BBC report that thirty-five members of the British Army liaison team in Kuwait, who like Clem were working for the Ministry of Defence, had been taken to Baghdad. There was worse to come. One of Clem's Pakistani colleagues told him that the Al Jaber airbase, where he worked, had been overrun. This was bad news. There were details of Clem and his address at the base and we were afraid he would be traced to our apartment. Then friends began calling to tell us that house-to-house searches for Westerners had begun in earnest. One said he had seen Iraqis enter the Al Muthana apartment complex where many Westerners lived. Sheila Chabowski, a Yugoslav friend married to an Englishman, told me a Frenchman had been held at a checkpoint. We also learnt that the German woman who had been raped and her husband were in Iraqi custody.

The BBC was broadcasting advice from the Foreign Office, telling Britons to stay indoors. The US State Department was telling Americans to leave the country, although they were not giving any hint as to how this might be achieved. In the early days of the invasion, such was the confusion outside that it would probably have been possible to find a way to the border. Many indeed did, either driving over sand tracks and keeping away from the main highway which ran in a straight line from Kuwait City to the border crossings of Nuwaisib or Wafra – a risky endeavour – or by taking a chance and just driving down the expressway in the hope that the Iraqis were too busy with their own dispositions to notice or care. Many of these escapes were made by Westerners living in close proximity to each other who quickly arranged their getaway in groups of four or six. We did not know any Westerners in our area and, in any case, the Iraqi troop concentration around us was one of the biggest in the city, and was a strong deterrent to even leaving the flat. The conflicting advice from Washington and London did not help, and the American and British embassies were not saying anything either.

Clem and I were in the mood to believe anything and nothing. When Sheila again called to tell us to expect an American attack that night we desperately wanted to believe her. I had known Sheila for about four years. She worked for one of the main advertising agencies and we would meet for lunch from time to time. Although we did not know each other too well, I enjoyed her company. We both shared Yugoslav origins but when she married Michael, who worked for a Kuwaiti trading company, she went out of her way to become fully anglicised. They had a four-year-old boy and lived in a villa in the popular suburb of Jabriya. In those first days after the invasion she seemed to know a lot about what was happening. We spoke several times a day. On many occasions she had news of what the Iraqis were currently doing. They were picking up foreigners; they were attacking a police station; she had the latest reports on shooting incidents. She had her own network of friends and she also risked regular trips to the Co-op across from her house. Each time she had something new to tell, she delivered it in hushed tones and confided that what she was telling me was highly secret and came from the most confidential of sources. Goodness knows what they were. I suppose it was because of her apparent inside knowledge that Clem and I were inclined to believe that she just might know more than we did and that an American attack could indeed be imminent.

My Palestinian friend Lima, from the newspaper, was another who seemed to know what was going on. She lived in Jabriya near Sheila and had many Kuwaiti and Arab friends. There was not much military activity around her home and she continued to go out. She also had a sister working at the Mubarak Hospital. Lima confirmed what I had earlier heard from my French friend, Michelle, that the hospital was still under Kuwaiti control. Michelle was concerned about her Indian husband Anindo Mukarjee who had a kidney disorder and relied on dialysis to survive. The Iraqis had already begun looting Kuwait's medical stores and she was afraid that there would be a shortage of dialysis fluid. They were later

33

forced to leave Kuwait with the Indian contingent to save his life. When Lima rang to ask if we had a basement to hide in, she too had heard the rumour that an American attack seemed likely.

We didn't have a basement but we were taking the possibility of an attack seriously. We were not sure what we were supposed to be preparing for. War? Or was it arrest, torture or worse? By now I felt the Iraqis would come before the Americans, and that it was only a question of time.

We decided to pack. Either the Iraqis would come or we would have to run for it. We didn't know which. I was more worried about leaving behind my things: my books, letters, pictures and clothes, my story cuttings. I suddenly saw big chunks of my life being wrenched from me: my past, my career, my memories. I flipped through my photographs and quickly placed into a separate album the pictures of my great-grandmother, my parents when they were young, and my sister and me when we were children.

I thought of my mother and recalled her telling me how she escaped in the Second World War through a window, leaving her mother to face the Gestapo who came to arrest her. In the past the story had seemed the stuff of fiction, now it became real, and I broke down in tears. I wasn't weeping about any one thing but all kinds of things crowded together. I know I was worried about Clem and me, and being separated from him. We weren't married and we were afraid that if the Iraqis came they would split us up and take us to different detention centres. It was a sobering moment; they would drag you out with one little bag or something and you wouldn't know where you were going or if you would ever see anyone you knew again. I felt that my life was falling apart.

Clem and I sat down and wrote powers of attorney: in case one of us stayed free we could draw money from the other's bank account. We exchanged contact addresses and vowed to get in touch with each other as soon as the crisis was over. Things had not been going too smoothly between Clem and I before the invasion. Yet at this moment all that seemed so stupid and trivial, and the thought of being forcibly torn from each other was unbearable.

At about noon the tanks and trucks rolled back up to the intersection near the Messilah Beach Hotel, just as they had on the first day, except this time they were going in the opposite direction. Could this be the promised withdrawal the Iraqis had earlier announced? But when all the vehicles moved away from the junction three hours later, we could see the checkpoint was still manned.

The Iraqis had announced the withdrawal worldwide and worldwide it was received with scepticism. The Western media and governments nevertheless were watching closely to see if Saddam would in this case keep his word, as he had on previous occasions in different circumstances. The deadline for the withdrawal was the next day, Sunday 5 August, the fourth day since the invasion.

I went to the sitting room. The aquarium was humming and the circulating water sounded as if there was a stream running through the room. The clock chiming was a comforting sound. I looked at the newspaper on the floor. It was the *Arab Times* dated July 26/27 and the headline read: 'It's Over'.

If only it were true.

V

There was something to be said for staying indoors, however cut off we felt. We had only pieces of the full picture, but they were enough to show us that if we were caught at the wrong place at the wrong time the consequences could be dire. Gun battles were still going on in various parts of the city and, if I had attempted to move as freely as I had before the invasion, I could easily have been caught in the crossfire.

It happened to Nirmala's brother. He was driving past the Central Bank on a tour of the city, to discover what was going on, when he saw a shootout between Iraqi soldiers and some gunmen across the road. He couldn't identify whether the others were Kuwaiti soldiers left behind, or civilians. He parked his car and ran for cover. When the shooting died down, he returned to his car to find a bullet lodged in one of his rear lights. He kept it as a souvenir.

As an Indian, he was safer than we Westerners. It was one of the ironies of the occupation that the once under-privileged Eastern expatriates were now in a better position than the Kuwaitis they had served in peacetime. They were not of much interest to Iraqis, and were able to move around freely without attracting much more than a passing glance. Moreover, there were so many of them – about 400,000 in total – they could merge into the scenery much more effectively than a Westerner. Nevertheless the situation of Eastern expatriates was anything but comfortable. Eastern women were often the victims of

36

Iraqi rapes and, because they tended to spend a lot of their earnings on jewellery, they were a prime target for thieves.

As it happened, Nirmala and her brother were our first visitors. Despite his experience, their account of life on the streets was more reassuring than we had dared hope. She had had no problems with the Iraqis she had encountered, she said, and had been rushing from one shop to another, stockpiling food, mineral water and cooking gas, while her brother had gone in search of petrol. She knew our food supplies were low and had brought us cans of tuna fish, corned beef and baked beans. We also got help from Mohammed, our Palestinian neighbour downstairs. But it was at a price. His ten cans of meat and vegetables, two dozen eggs, a kilo of white beans and one of black-eyed peas cost $29, double the pre-invasion price.

Mohammed and his wife were born in Kuwait but, like most Palestinians, had no right of residence and, even before the invasion, might have been expelled for the slightest offence. He told me: 'It is all right for you. You have a country to go to. If we have to leave Kuwait, where do we go?'

Another man who felt his career had been nipped in the bud by the invasion was Omar Korshed, a Palestinian with American citizenship. He had arrived in Kuwait only three weeks before to work as a landscape architect at the Kuwait Institute for Scientific Research. This was his first job since college. He lived with his father in a villa along the road from us and was desperate to leave Kuwait. He came to see Clem to inquire if he had managed to get in touch with the American Embassy.

Clem's Pakistani workmate Ahmed was equally gloomy about his job prospects if the Iraqis maintained control of the country: 'The Iraqis don't need advisers. They'll only keep the domestic servants,' he said. Ahmed was thinking of putting his name down for evacuation by the ships Pakistan had said it was sending to carry off 80,000 of its people working in Kuwait. The ships never came.

Stories of evacuations were gathering momentum. We heard the Austrian and Swiss embassies had notified their nationals to report and to be ready to leave. There was, however, no word from the British and Americans. To our knowledge, nothing had yet been organised or was even being contemplated.

With others talking about their losses and prospects, we began to consider our own. Apart from our jobs, our losses could be counted in purely material terms: the money in the bank, our furniture and our personal belongings. By now, none of that mattered; all either of us cared about was getting out unhurt.

We told ourselves we could always start over again somewhere else. Clem even remembered a job he had turned down a few months before with the UAE Air Force in the Emirates. I was, anyway, bored with life on the *Arab Times* and had been preparing to return to England later in the year. But, without a job, I had kept postponing my departure. With the experience of this crisis, I felt more hopeful. We were both reasonably optimistic when we discussed our prospects, and looking forward, into the future, perked us up. We left unspoken the fact that taking the options we were discussing would lead to our separation. If we left Kuwait we would be heading for different destinations. Whatever we thought, we preferred not to speak about it. Our relationship, which had in recent months stuttered in fits and starts, was now momentarily cemented by the crisis. There were too many more immediate things to think about.

There was an increasing danger from looters, not only

because we could lose our possessions, but also because it was in their interests to alert the authorities to our presence. If the looters could get us arrested, the house would be left empty and the way clear for them to take what they wanted.

Goran Stojkovic, a Yugoslav engineer in Jabriya, called to say that troops had entered a flat in Al Muthana complex. Its American occupants got off lightly, though. The Iraqis had only asked to see their identity cards and had not detained them. They did, however, take a fancy to a painting and took it with them when they left. Goran saw some of the looting in the gold souk when a squad of soldiers drove up and systematically carried out all the gold from the shops. They stacked it neatly inside the truck and drove away. Whether this was an official or a private heist, he did not know. Two Palestinian boys took a leaf out of the Iraqis' book by breaking into the Kuwait Bookshop in Salmiya and walking away with the cash register. On the other side of the same street, the Alba watch store was stripped clean and the Rolls Royce showroom nearby was emptied of all its newest models.

To counter the looting in some areas, the Kuwaitis organised vigilante groups. They were led by ex-policemen and soldiers who were used to handling weapons. Leaflets were also distributed, appealing to Kuwaitis not to hoard, to be sparing with electricity and water and to ignore rumours put about by the Iraqis. From this it was apparent that a resistance movement of sorts had been formed and armed Kuwaitis had already begun patrolling the streets of Kheifan to the west of the city. It was never clear how co-ordinated the movement was; it seemed more likely that individual groups had got together in various parts of the city and organised their own cells, carrying out attacks on troops and storage depots where and when they could locate them. Much of the shooting that we heard after the first few days was exchanges of fire between these groups and Iraqi troops.

The rapid withdrawal of the Kuwaiti Army on the first day of the invasion, and the absence of any signs of the heavy weaponry and armour the Kuwaiti forces possessed, suggested to most people that not only had they been taken by surprise but also no command structure was in place to organise effective resistance. I did not see a single Kuwaiti plane in the skies and neither, as far as I know, did anyone else. Later reports that Kuwaiti planes had attacked Iraqi positions from their bases in Bahrain, and that Kuwaiti Mirage aircraft had managed to escape to Saudi Arabia, suggested a rapid retreat with the intention of preserving as much of the air force and army as possible, to enable them to fight another day. Six months later, this turned out to be the case.

At our home, the soldiers now seemed to have disappeared from across the road and although the checkpoint was still in place at the intersection, it now seemed a long way off, though it was, in fact, only a short sprint. I took the rubbish out that night. It was quiet and warm outside and it felt good. The street was deserted, except for the cats that had proliferated around the building and were scavenging for any scraps they could find. I did not stay long, afraid I might be spotted by soldiers on night patrol, and hurried back inside.

Clem was cooking dinner. He was well known among his friends for his muffins, which he managed to turn out at lightning speed. We had always shared the work around the flat. I washed the dishes and he did the cooking. I knew that cooking helped him work out some of his frustrations and killed the boredom. Being cooped up in the apartment didn't bother me unduly, but I felt sorry for Clem because he is such an active outdoors person. Since the invasion he had mostly slept and watched movies on the video recorder. Performing household chores was one of the few activities that hadn't been changed by the invasion and allowed us to maintain at least a semblance of normality. My other duties were to monitor Iraqi movements and answer the phone.

It seemed a miracle the phones were still working inside the city, but that was because the Iraqis needed them as much as we did. What we would have done without the phone, heaven knows. It sustained me throughout the occupation and, although lines sometimes got crossed, the system never failed once until almost the last day of the war. In these early days of the invasion it was our only window on to the turbulent world outside.

When we heard that an Iraqi helicopter had crashed in Hawalli it gave us something to cheer about. This was followed by rumours of the assassination of Saddam Hussein and then a coup in Baghdad. We doubted any of it were true but, for want of more definite information, it seemed something to celebrate. Normally it would have been an occasion to toast in wine but that was part of our staple diet anyway, as it was for most other Western expatriates. The shelves of the supermarkets were always being emptied of grape juice by people who made their own wine in plastic dustbins. In pre-invasion days liquor was illegal, but the authorities had turned a blind eye to home-brewing. As a quasi-secular state, Iraq had a much more relaxed attitude to liquor and, after the invasion, it came flowing into Kuwait. In the wake of the troops, the Iraqi traders came in their droves, selling vegetables and cigarettes but mostly beer and spirits. They would stand on street corners, in full view of the troops. The liquor would be camouflaged by their other wares piled on the pavement beside them. A case of beer cost $75 and a bottle of whisky about $55. This was a fraction of the price on the black market before the invasion and some expatriates took full advantage of it. Some I knew and many I heard about drank heavily while in hiding. Getting through the crisis in a half-drunken stupor blunted the senses and helped them survive.

When it was first announced that Iraqi traders would be coming to Kuwait to sell foodstuffs, it was good news for most of us. Huge stocks of food had been seized in army raids on shops in the city and shipped back to Iraq. We were hoping that some of it was now being returned. Instead, what happened was that Iraqi farmers were allowed to bring in their produce. It did not exactly provide for a varied diet. For the next two months the only plentiful foodstuffs were watermelons and onions.

Many a night we sat watching TV, nursing a glass of whisky while watching the news from outside. We could pick up TV from Dubai and Saudi Arabia, Qatar and Bahrain. The coverage of the invasion was conspicuously low-key for the first few days, probably because they were hoping for a quick Arab solution and did not want to antagonise the Iraqis. At that time they were placing great hopes on a summit that was to have brought Saddam and the Amir together in Riyadh. It never took place and soon the news coverage was increasing its hostility to Saddam and his invaders. With Kuwait TV in the hands of the Iraqis, we were effectively watching Baghdad Television. Saddam's dapper spokesman became as familiar to us as he was to viewers in London, Paris and Washington. The mere mention of Saddam's name by this time was enough to turn our stomachs and we regarded him as lower than vermin. We became particularly cynical when he changed his uniform into civilian clothes to project a softer image.

The embassies, meanwhile, were still not accessible.

Phones were not answered or lines were busy. Some were cut. That Sunday evening, however, provided one ray of hope. The BBC began urging Britons to get in touch with the embassy on any one of four numbers that were broadcast. I tried the first and couldn't get through but when I dialled the second, a woman answered and took my name and phone number. She said the embassy was preparing an evacuation and I should stay tuned to the BBC. It wasn't much but it was something – at least they were aware I was among their community.

We were all, I suppose, becoming a bit melodramatic. Sheila called and in her cryptic way again implied that another American attack was expected that night. We had already heard from other friends that Iraqi guns and tanks were trained on the Gulf and she advised: 'Turn one room into a shelter.' Then she abruptly put the phone down. Given my volatile state, I became alarmed again. It felt as if I had to change up into a higher gear, and my heart began racing and my hands trembled. I felt utterly sick.

We were totally unprepared for any sort of attack and felt horribly exposed. Our flat was only 100 metres from the beach and one shell would have obliterated us. The Iraqi encampment near the Messilah Beach Hotel was an obvious target and, in any attack, we would be in the direct line of fire.

I tried to persuade Clem to prepare for the worst. First we should get dressed and have our bags packed with basic essentials. Then we should try to block a window in one of the rooms with furniture, move in the dining table and hide under it. I also thought we should sleep in shifts. Clem looked at me as if I were insane. Not only did he refuse to co-operate, but he got furious with me for panicking.

43

'The best thing is to keep cool,' he said and fatalistically added, 'What has to happen, will happen.'

I must admit he practised what he preached. He walked around in his underpants all day, munching muffins and looking bored. He would then sleep for hours. I had to admire how composed and unperturbed he had seemed from the beginning. I wasn't. From the very start my emotions were very close to the surface. He also frequently wanted to make love, which I thought insane. We had a row. I lay in my jeans and sweatshirt and turned my back on him. I felt sleep was more of a priority if I was to preserve my strength. In many ways it was a classic breakdown in communication. I showed my fear, Clem didn't – which is not to say that he wasn't as fearful as I was inside. He went some way towards comforting me when I needed it but when it turned sexual, I became angry. He probably thought that while I was seeking comfort from him, I was not prepared to return it in the way he wanted. Later on in the crisis, similar views were expressed by other people caught in the turmoil. Almost without exception, the women had been turned off sex and the men turned on. The men seemed to respond to the violence around them with a heightened libido while, for the women, the opposite was the case. It was significant that as the violence diminished – or as we became more accustomed to it – our feelings returned to something like normal.

That night I was in no mood to analyse and, still with my back to Clem, dropped off to sleep. In fact it was not much more than a nap. I woke at about 3 a.m. and sat by the sitting-room window. The streetlights were on and I could see the soldiers at the Messilah intersection chatting and smoking under the warm night sky. The curfew was on and every now and then a military truck or jeep drove past. It was daybreak when I returned to

44

bed in the belief that any immediate danger had passed and that we could relax, at least until dusk. How wrong I was.

VI

Boiled egg and toast for breakfast. Last night was last night and I felt almost as good as new this morning. It seemed now as if I could use fear to recycle my energy. But my hold on a sense of well-being was very tenuous. I only had to look out of our window to see the soldiers across the road, and the threat staring me in the face.

Clem was also in a good mood. We always quarrelled and made up very fast. So I knew it was concern for me which prompted his suggestion that I might move to a safer place without him. That way, he thought, I would stand a better chance of escaping arrest. But, as far as I was concerned, the idea was out of the question. To leave without him in order to save my own skin would be the ultimate act of betrayal. I was horrified by any such suggestion. As it happened my Indian colleague Fathima called to suggest both of us should move to her place in Farwaniya, on the way to the airport; an area largely populated by Arabs and Indians.

I told her that Clem had urged me to move but I didn't think it was fair.

'This is no time to talk about what's fair,' she said. I did not argue but I did bristle.

We were committed to seeing it through together and we set about converting our spare bedroom into a shelter. We took the double bed apart and barricaded the window. This made me feel more at ease. We were doing something; we were at least trying to help ourselves. There wasn't much more we could do.

My Yugoslav friend Goran called and said the Sultan Centre in Salmiya was full of Westerners shopping; they were mainly Britons. One of them had shrugged off any talk of the threat saying: 'The Iraqis are only after people in uniform.' We soon learned differently. Clem found out from a company contact that the Iraqis had now begun picking up Westerners from the hotels and arranging for them to be taken to Baghdad. Clem was told to stay put but I was afraid they might start searching houses any time. The Yugoslav Embassy had told its nationals to move into the chancery in Shamiya and to bring their own food and water with them. My American editor on the *Arab Times*, Tadeusz 'Ski' Karwecki, had made inquiries and found that only the guests at the Messilah Beach had been picked up. Ski was thirty-eight, and a widely travelled journalist. He had worked in Japan, where he met his wife, and before coming to Kuwait had spent eight years on a newspaper in Saudi Arabia. He was a quiet, self-contained person but, despite working with him for nearly two years, I can't say I knew him well. He did not mix a great deal socially and spent a lot of time at the office. I had met his wife Ikuko by chance once while shopping in a supermarket. They lived in a small apartment in Jabriya. When I told him how scared I was about the amount of Iraqi activity around us, he immediately said that Clem and I were welcome to stay with him and his wife. While I had never thought of him as anything but an extremely decent person, this generous gesture came as something of a surprise.

Ski had sowed the idea in my mind and I was now set upon moving. I thought it would be better to move in with somebody I knew well and the first person to come to mind was Sheila. We had been in constant touch over the phone and we always got on well when we met. I called her and put it to her straight. She seemed enthusiastic: 'Yes, please come, no problem.' I explained about Clem being a potential target because of his connections with the Ministry of Defence. Was she sure it was all right if he came with me? She said: 'Of course, bring Clem.'

Clem tried to check out his colleague at the Messilah Hotel to see if he had been picked up but could not get through. I told him about Sheila's invitation.

'I'm not going anywhere,' he said. I was near despair. I felt danger creeping ever closer. There were too many soldiers around and we were sitting ducks. Every morning they were on the doorstep of the apartment block, asking for food. How much longer could the Palestinians downstairs keep them from coming up, especially as they were now actively seeking out Westerners. If we ventured out, we risked being detained on the street, but I felt it was a risk worth taking. Clem could pass for a Sudanese and I had my Yugoslav passport. It was no longer valid, but would they look that closely at it, and would they be looking to arrest a woman? I doubted it.

The only emotion Clem displayed was irritation with my pleadings. It took a phone call to another of his workmates, who told him, 'It might be a good idea to move.'

So it was decided.

I began racing around, packing whatever came to hand. We did not know whether we would ever come back to the flat. Clem packed the food, one can at a time, then the frozen stuff, rice and onions. He was so slow, it nearly drove me into a frenzy. I grabbed Matzi, the kitten that I had rescued from the press room at the newspaper a month before, and we finally left the building. First we checked the street. It looked deserted. From ground level we were unable to see the soldiers at the intersection, but neither could they see us. We went out and began to load up the car. The heat was fierce and the car, a 1985 Mitsubishi Gallant, was like an oven.

We were setting off when Clem decided to pop in to our Palestinian neighbours' flat to get their phone number. The kitten was struggling in my arms and I was trying to hold a bag at the same time. The whole situation was absurd. I was about to get into the car when I glanced down the road and saw a group of about six soldiers coming towards me. They were barely 50 metres away and I stood frozen to the spot. I wanted to run back inside as fast as I could. The front door was only ten steps away. I don't know what held me back, but I tried to look casual. I closed the door of the car and turned the key in the lock. Averting my face from the soldiers to avoid eye contact, and resisting the urge to break into a sprint, I walked slowly to the gate, across the yard, up the few steps and through the front door. I let out a breath and shouted Clem's name at the same time. He came out of the neighbours' flat and I told him what I had seen. We rushed upstairs to our flat and locked the door. From behind the curtains, we watched the soldiers enter the building. I was sure they had come for us and was beside myself. I ran from the door to the window and back. I could hear loud voices below. I wanted to call someone, anyone, to let them know what was happening, but my telephone book was in the car. I sat by the phone, silently screaming, because I could not remember a single number.

Then, as if I had willed it, the phone rang. I grabbed it. It was Omar from down the road. He, too, had seen the soldiers and was watching them from his window.

'Don't worry,' he said. 'All they want are the cars.'

I hoped that was all they wanted. I rushed back to Clem and told him if they asked for the car he should give them the keys to his Fifth Avenue. He said he would do no such thing.

My head was spinning. Why couldn't Clem compromise? The voices from downstairs were getting louder and the kitten was mewing like mad. All of a sudden, I couldn't breathe properly. I was hyperventilating.

The phone rang again. It was Omar. They had gone, he said. He had seen them turn the corner. But I could still hear an argument going on downstairs. It was the neighbours, deep in discussion. They had forgotten to tell us the danger had passed. The soldiers, they later told us, had wanted food and water and had become somewhat aggressive about it. I was now convinced the sooner we left this place, the better.

This time Clem agreed. We returned to the car and instantly had an argument about who would drive. I was already behind the wheel, but Clem thought that it would be less conspicuous if he drove. But I had by this time started the engine. He started complaining: it was bad luck he had been caught in this situation with me, he said. That hurt, but I kept quiet and soon I was driving at 85 kmph down the Fahaheel expressway; the road that leads to the Saudi border though we were going in the opposite direction. We were heading for Sheila's in Jabriya. On the way we passed many army vehicles and groups of soldiers, as I had done on my first trip out. I noticed the CID building had been blackened by fire and the watchtowers on the Bayan Palace were scarred from shellfire. The roads were again marked with the prints of the tank tracks, and the Jabriya police station was also in bad shape and had been abandoned. On some wasteland I saw a man selling fruit from the bonnet of his car. We turned right off the highway and pulled up in front of their house. What a relief! It was Clem's first trip out and I could tell he was tense, but he didn't say anything because we'd had the argument over who should drive.

Our clothes were drenched with sweat and the kitten, who was sitting in the back, was soaking wet when I picked it up. Michael, Sheila's husband, met us at the door. Inside it was cool and we were among friends. It was such a relief to have arrived intact and to be with other people again. I talked excitedly about everything that had been happening to us. Sheila and her Filipino maid gave us coffee and we talked as Sheila prepared lunch and her little boy played with the kitten. The family atmosphere was so comforting. By the time we had finished eating, I felt smug with contentment. I did not underestimate what was going on outside, but now felt that collectively we could all cope much better.

It was not to be. At about 7.30 in the evening Safet, a Yugoslav baker, braved the curfew to bring us bread and bad news. He had just seen a convoy of more than a hundred cars driven by Iraqi soldiers advancing towards Jabriya. Sheila began making frantic phone calls and asked one of her husband's business friends to send Salah to stay the night. He was known to the family and was streetwise. When it was finally confirmed he was on his way Sheila calmed down. She was awaiting his arrival in the darkness by the window when she suddenly cried 'Soldiers!' Half a dozen of them were crossing the school parking lot towards the villa.

'They are coming, they are coming,' said Sheila. She was extremely agitated and so were the rest of us. The soldiers split into two groups, three of them coming our way. That dreadful feeling rose up in me again. I leaned against the wall in the sitting room, folded my arms and rocked from my waist back and forth, breathing short deep breaths. I was afraid I would hyperventilate again. Then I heard Sheila say excitedly: 'There is Salah! Thank God!' Then there was a pause: 'What is he doing? Oh, my God, he doesn't know where we live. He's gone right past the gate . . . What's the matter with him? Who is he talking to? Oh, no, he is talking to the soldiers. Oh no, the fool!'

She jumped from the settee and rushed outside. 'Salah!' she screamed. She returned a minute or two later, looking composed again. She was accompanied by a man in a white coat. Salah had curly black hair, a narrow face, droopy but sharp eyes, and a big nose. He looked familiar and he said he was Doctor Salah. He shook hands with everyone. Michael knew him well, and Clem also seemed to recognise him.

We all sat on the floor in the dimly lit living room, sipped coffee and smoked. Salah told us a stream of stories of how he had rescued Kuwaitis from Iraqis who took over the Military Training College in Reggai, which was some way to the north of the city. As a doctor, he said, he had gone to attend the wounded. He didn't seem to have any fear of the Iraqis and when we asked him about them he said: 'No problem. You saw me out there. I just went up to them and talked.'

We listened to the BBC news and discovered more than four hundred Britons and Americans were now being held in Baghdad. At one point, Sheila, remembering Clem, exclaimed: 'Oh, my God, Clem is a military man!' She had known all along where he had worked, but it seemed that it suddenly dawned on her that he, and possibly I, would be putting her and her family at risk. She was hospitable enough, but I noticed an edge in her voice. I felt she had begun to realise our presence would not make things easier. Salah reassured all of us. 'If the soldiers come, I will tell them this is my house. I'll say the maid is my wife and the rest of you can hide.'

In the absence of any better plan, we agreed. Salah was something of a hero and it was a role he obviously relished. About halfway through the evening I remembered where I had seen him before. He was no doctor; he was the caterer who had looked after the food for our New Year's party.

We had a restless night sleeping fully dressed on mattresses in the spare room. The phone was in there and it didn't stop ringing the whole night. Next morning, Sheila's friends began visiting. Some of them were investigating ways to escape to Saudi Arabia. But the driver they had sent to test the route returned with the news that the Iraqis had closed the frontier. Her friends urged Sheila to move to another villa with a basement but she was visibly shaken and couldn't decide what to do. 'I am afraid I'll never see my friends again,' she sobbed. I tried to comfort her and told her this was not the time to worry.

'Yes, it is,' her husband chipped in. 'Any time is the time to worry these days,' he said.

He put his arms around Sheila and led her to the bedroom. He was right. This was the right time to worry. The stress was taking its toll on all of us and I made a mental note to guard against sliding into a depression. Watching others crack up was somehow instructive, although I had done my share.

During the day, I began to feel uncomfortable. Sheila was extremely tense. Salah's boss, Sameer, a Lebanese with Australian citizenship, arrived with what sounded like an ambitious plan to get us new identity cards. They were to be forged on official hospital forms. We gave him what passport pictures we had with us and only two hours later he was back with the forged IDs. He said Sheila and I would not need them because of our Yugoslav passports. Michael's identified him as Polish and Clem's gave his name as Samuel Tambo, a Nigerian administrator at the maternity hospital. Clem knew nothing about Nigeria so we all set about educating him. We told him the name of the capital, and the name of the president, and Clem jotted it down while trying to commit it to memory.

Sameer then took Sheila and Michael aside to the master bedroom. Soon she called me. 'I don't know how to say this, but I don't think we are safe with Clem around.'

I felt my stomach drop, but I fought to keep control. I was determined not to show my disappointment. 'No problem, we'll go,' I said in a voice more calm than I felt.

Sameer then spoke. 'Not you, only him,' he said. 'For your own safety you should stay here.'

There was no way I was going to leave Clem. We had a chat in private and another row. He wanted to return to the flat. I felt it wasn't safe. I called Ski from Sheila's. He lived close by and when I asked if we could come and stay he said they would be happy to have us.

I tried to understand Sheila's attitude. She had a small son to think of, and she was obviously frightened, yet I still couldn't help feeling she had let us down. I wasn't bitter, and I sensed that we would stay in touch, but I did think that, in future, there would be a limit to our friendship.

In the living room Salah, who had been so talkative the night before, had been strangely quiet since Sameer arrived. Sameer seemed to treat him like an errand boy. Salah's face became sullen and he looked resentful. He was something of an enigma to me. I took his stories with a pinch of salt – but there was still something about him I couldn't quite pinpoint. The night before he had seemed just too comfortable with the Iraqis. Now, as we were about to go, he watched us silently, yet for a moment I even felt he was sympathising with us. But I was too

54

preoccupied with our next move to dwell for long on Salah. All I knew was that our road to safety was becoming increasingly bumpy.

VII

Ski and Ikuko lived on the fifth floor of an apartment block giving a wide view of the whole Jabriya area and, on the first night, we watched columns of smoke and the glow of a fire just across the highway. It was in Hawalli, where the main Palestinian community lived. Compared to our closeness to recent events, the fire, although only in the neighbouring district, still seemed wonderfully far away. Being here was a whole new way of life for us and much less stressful than the one we had left behind. There was little sign of any military presence and no soldiers ever came to the building.

Our stay began on a refreshingly upbeat note. The State Department issued a statement, relayed to us by one of Clem's workmates. It mentioned a multinational effort to evacuate foreigners, and, although there was no precise plan, we thought something was in the offing. It was our first clear communication from the US government and my spirits rose. We were not forgotten. The message also seemed to make sense of remarks made earlier that day by President Bush when he was asked in Washington what the American response to the crisis in Kuwait was going to be.

'Wait, watch and learn,' he said. Was the evacuation plan part of the President's message?

We called all our friends to tell them the news. We were, at the time, clinging to any remotely hopeful scrap of information and almost always shared it with others. I began to imagine a massive evacuation in which we would be lifted to safety by helicopters in a swirl of dust. The reality, I thought, would more likely be an arduous journey by road and so I decided to fill up my car with petrol. For this, I enlisted Goran's help. As a Yugoslav he had been moving around freely and we drove together to a petrol station a short distance away. We found a queue supervised by some young Kuwaitis. They were checking to make sure that only cars with tanks less than half full were allowed to fill up.

On an impulse, I decided to return to our old flat to collect some more of my things. All I had with me was my laptop computer, the family photo album, a couple of pairs of trousers, and three T-shirts. If we were to be evacuated, I wanted to take more stuff with me. We arrived to find the area deserted.

It felt strange being in the apartment again, eerily quiet and dark. Goran gave me fifteen minutes. There was so much I wanted to take and I started with a jar of coffee, some shoes and clothes. Then vanity got the better of me and I packed some perfume, costume jewellery and shampoo. I scurried around picking up this, discarding that, and stuffing all manner of small things into the pockets of my jeans. I felt like a thief in my own house. The fish in the aquarium looked none the worse for our absence. As a reward, I dropped a couple of food pellets into the water. That would keep them going for another couple of weeks.

On the way back we saw smoke rising from the CID building which we had seen damaged when we had passed on our way to Sheila's. The roads were almost free of all but military traffic. I was almost getting used to that. It was as hot as ever outside, but it didn't bother me. There were few signs of any major destruction, although there was a lot of litter in the streets, as if a sudden wind had swept across the city. Paper flew around the road, a slab of paving stone had been crushed to pieces, and every now and then we passed the wreck of a car, but there were still no military checkpoints to be seen.

It was August 8, almost a week since the invasion, and President Bush and Saddam were both due to speak. We waited eagerly to hear what they would have to say and our hopes were lifted after Iraqi TV displayed peace slogans while filming celebrations of the second anniversary of the end of the war with Iran. We even hoped Saddam might announce a real withdrawal. But President Bush's speech proved to be a colossal letdown. Our release was well down the list of conditions for solving the crisis, after an unconditional withdrawal, the return of the legitimate Kuwaiti government, and a new security arrangement for the area. The President at least acknowledged we were hostages; Saddam went further. He annexed Kuwait, making it Iraq's 19th Province, and in so doing, converted us all into residents of Iraq. It may have been a technicality, but we were gravely insulted.

Later that evening came the news that the Iraqis had moved missiles with chemical warheads into Kuwait. I was alarmed and the only way I could cope with the prospect of a chemical attack was to do something about protecting us. I seemed to need to respond to every Iraqi move with a counter-move of my own. It was almost as if I were defending a chess game. I was simply unable to take anything passively and, ever since the crisis began, I had felt that I was not only responsible for myself but also for those around me, above all Clem.

Ikuko and I began to devise a plan. We cut up plastic carrier bags and stuck them on one side of each of the airconditioning outlets. Then all that was necessary in an emergency would be to fix them on the wall. There was no shortage of advice from friends, although the means at our disposal were pitifully inadequate. Ikuko's Japanese friends advised us to switch off the airconditioning. Sheila called to say we should prepare wet towels. Someone else told us that poison gas would not be a serious hazard because we were on the fifth floor; it was a heavy gas and would tend to descend quickly. Goran, sensible as ever, said that if the Iraqis had wanted to gas us they would hardly have brought their missiles to Kuwait when they could fire them from Iraq.

Ikuko and I were deaf to such advice and continued to work on our plastic bags. We decided that in the event of a gas attack we should huddle together in a small windowless hallway in the centre of the flat. It had doors on three sides but only an arched passageway to the sitting room. We taped some newspapers together and made a curtain to hang as a door. Then we scrapped the whole idea and decided the bathroom was the best place. Its tiny window was already taped to prevent the dust from coming in, and there was also water on hand.

The next day, the Japanese Embassy called, advising Ikuko to move into the embassy. About two hundred Japanese had already moved in, among them Ikuko's friend Mika who was married to a Kuwaiti, Abdul Latif Shamali. Mika spent her nights in the chancery basement and her husband would pick her up in the morning and take her home. Ikuko, however, was in no mood to heed her embassy's advice. When she had first been phoned soon after the invasion, the embassy had flatly refused to allow Ski to accompany her.

'I am from a Samurai family and I will not beg them to take my husband,' she fumed. But this time the embassy was willing to bend the rules. She could bring her husband along, but no friends.

I wanted them to feel free to go. I was sure we could take care of ourselves, but Ikuko scoffed at the idea.

'Tell them that when the moment comes for an evacuation, we'll be there,' Ski told Ikuko. She had earlier rejected a Japanese scheme for an evacuation to Saudi Arabia that, in the end, never materialised.

Ski, concerned for her safety, wanted her to leave with the Japanese. He thought she stood a better chance with her own people than with him, an American.

'I will roll you up in a bundle, tie and gag you, and put you on a truck. You can scream as much as you want when you get to Saudi Arabia,' he told her.

'I'd rather die in the comfort of my own home than in the desert or the embassy,' she said.

The plan fell through when the embassy found it could only get hold of seven vans to carry two hundred people.

The Japanese hinted that something else might be in the offing. We were intrigued and didn't want to take any chances if they had received some advance notice of an American attack. While I waited for Sameer to bring over food, Ikuko went to inspect a bomb shelter in a basement of a neighbouring block. It was a big place and had water connected. Some Britons, always the better organised for such emergencies, had already booked their places. We debated whether to spend the night in there, and I packed a small bag. We also arranged to take cushions to sleep on but just as we were about to make the final decision, Clem clutched his arm suddenly. 'I feel ill,' he said. A sharp pain had swept up his left arm and into his chest. I was terrified. I thought: 'He's having a heart attack.'

Clem is an exceptionally active and energetic man but he was overweight and he had a history of high blood pressure. While he lay on the bed we discussed what to do. It was a bad time to fall sick. The curfew was on and the clinics were under Iraqi control. Even if he went to hospital, the Iraqis might take him captive. But saving his life was more important, so we were ready to do whatever necessary.

We thought of taking him to the US Embassy where scores of Americans had gone into hiding and we were sure there must be a doctor. Ski called Bill Van Rye, an American banker who took it upon himself to keep US citizens in touch with each other and their embassy. He knew of an Arab who would drive Clem through the checkpoints. We decided to wait for a while. Every now and then I checked on him. He said the pain was still there, but when I went to the bedroom later, he did not speak. He was absolutely still.

'My God, he's dead,' I thought. I put my ear to his face, he was breathing and in a deep sleep. What a relief! I wanted to hug and kiss him, but refrained in case I woke him. It later turned out he had suffered an attack of gastritis.

Our domestic life was unfolding against the background of sporadic rifle fire and explosions. We never quite knew whether it was the resistance movement on sabotage missions or the Iraqis blowing up buildings or shooting Kuwaitis. Every time we heard the noise we would pick up the phone and dial someone to try to find out. Few were any wiser than we were.

At about noon on August 10 there was a big bang not far from our block. We saw some commotion in the traffic on the main road but little else. Lima later told us that the Iraqis had found a car spattered with bullet holes. They thought it must have been used in a hit-and-run attack by the resistance and blew it up. Lima also told us about a demonstration by women in front of the Jabriya Co-op. They were shielding a sniper who suddenly opened fire on some Iraqi soldiers. The soldiers returned the fire and mowed down ten women. While I admired the bravery of the women, I couldn't help thinking of the futility of it. Their gesture did not amount to a pinprick to the Iraqi forces, but I supposed it was the gesture that counted.

Mika's husband confirmed the resistance had, as we had thought, begun on day one, mainly carrying out symbolic raids to boost morale. Many burnt-out tanks and army vehicles, some of which may have been the ones I had seen on the roadsides, had been among the targets of the resistance. There were also reports of Iraqi soldiers having been killed and their bodies found overnight in roadside refuse containers.

VIII

While we mouthed sympathy for the plight of the Kuwaitis, in the beginning we were all basically motivated by self-interest; all we wanted to do was get out. It was not our country and it conveniently slipped our minds that we had been living off its fat. But as time went by, our attitudes changed, until we felt a close affinity with the Kuwaitis and, indeed, they with us. We were all in it together and it was a bit like sharing a lifeboat. Nationality ceased to matter.

It was around this time that Demirok called to say the Yugoslavs were making preparations to evacuate their people. Goran confirmed that a convoy was preparing to leave. My instinctive reaction was to stay in Kuwait but I could visualise my parents searching for me when the Yugoslav refugees arrived in Belgrade. I could imagine their disappointment and anxiety if I were not with the convoy. Not for the first time, such a thought made me shed a few tears. I stared at the pictures in my family album. My parents were young and smiling, with my elder sister Vanja and me. In the background was the monastery of St Naum beside Lake Ohrid in southern Macedonia. We had last been there in 1952, when I was two. There was a picture of my father in the uniform of a pre-Second World War army officer. Others were of my mother looking sportive in riding boots, and gentle as a nurse. There were a lot of photos of Vanja and me dressed like twins, although she is almost two years older than I. I wanted to be a little girl once more, protected, secure and loved, and for the first time I wondered if I would ever see my family again.

My sentimental meanderings were ended abruptly by an explosion that shook the whole area. An Iraqi armoured carrier had been blown up by the resistance. It was an event that, I suppose, was crucial in helping me to make a decision about staying or leaving Kuwait. I decided to stay, at least for the time being. There would be other convoys.

I now had to get a valid Yugoslav passport which would relieve me of the hazard of being British and allow me to get out and about; the East Europeans were moving around freely and, as part of the Eastern Bloc, had been Iraqi allies during the Cold War. I asked Goran to drive me to the embassy in the city centre, not far from the Sheraton roundabout.

It was a nerve-racking drive and, on the way, we saw troops driving around in civilian pick-up trucks, their rifles sticking out of the windows. The roundabout itself was a mess. An abandoned red truck with Iraqi licence plates, its bonnet open, stood in the centre of the grass. There were wrecked cars everywhere and sewage had flooded over one section. What was once something of a design showpiece now looked like a place that had been abused by squatters, which, I suppose, was precisely what the Iraqis were. I was almost as surprised to see pictures of the Amir and the Prime Minister still sticking to the walls and fences beside the main road. The Iraqis had not yet got around to removing them.

The Yugoslav Embassy looked like a refugee camp. It was packed with people. There were men stripped to the waist, lounging in the gardens with sweat streaming down their backs. Inside the building, bags, suitcases and all manner of luggage was thrown everywhere, with men and women stretched out on mattresses on the floor.

Children were running to and fro, some laughing, some crying. Some screeching parrots added to the general din.

'Shut those bloody parrots up,' someone shouted.

'We can't, they belong to the ambassador,' was the reply.

I ran upstairs to what used to be the ambassador's office, and knocked on the door. It was opened by the counsellor Dako Ostojic. His wife was inside with him, looking neat and fresh, and their daughter, who looked about twelve, was lying asleep on a sofa. They had been on leave in Yugoslavia when he was ordered to return to Kuwait just after the invasion. They had driven overland from Belgrade, stopping over in Baghdad, where he said everyone was in jubilant mood. He had no inkling of the chaos in Kuwait.

He was worried about Vesna Pardo, a Yugoslav who had not been seen since the invasion. She was a physio-therapist who had treated members of the royal family and he thought she might have been in the Dasman Palace when it was attacked, but the Iraqis had assured him that they had given those in the Palace plenty of time to leave before shelling it. They thought Vesna may have fled with the Al Sabah family.

I went downstairs to get my new passport. There was a huge crowd and Verica, a clerk in her late thirties, and normally a calm, self-possessed woman, was up to her neck in work. She was answering phones, puffing at a cigarette, filling in forms, rebuking her young son and ordering her husband about, all at the same time. Her right arm was held out to a doctor who was taking her blood pressure. She explained – unnecessarily – 'I am at the end of my tether.'

I got my passport and couldn't wait to get out of the building. I was now glad I had decided not to join their convoy. I felt more secure with a valid passport in my

65

pocket and I headed with new resolve back to Jabriya.

The news was bad. Two of Clem's workmates had left without telling him. It was a severe blow to our morale and I seethed. While there was no love lost between Clem and many of his workmates, I thought they should have put petty personal differences aside under these circumstances.

Clem was the only black man on the staff and he felt it. Most of the Americans were retired US Air Force and Navy officers. Clem had been hired mainly because the Kuwaitis wanted him. He had a Ph.D. in education and, because of his Air Force background, they wanted him to develop their Air Force training programme. Unlike some of his colleagues, Clem got on well with the Kuwaitis and, on at least one occasion, he was used to smooth over difficulties with them.

On the day of the invasion his boss in Kuwait was away on vacation. An ex-navy pilot, John Cox, took over and it was he who had called us early on that first morning. When the phone link to the south was cut, an ex-colonel took charge. He was in radio contact with the US Embassy and, in the early days of the invasion, he burnt documents and records of the people working for their company in its offices in Salmiya. He lived in a villa not far away and, after the invasion, some of Clem's workmates moved in with him. Two days before they left, one of them phoned Clem to ask if he had a map of Kuwait, but he made no mention of any escape attempt. The American who told us about it said several of the company's workers had made it to the Saudi border in four-wheel-drive jeeps. When Clem expressed his disappointment at not having been told, the man agreed. It was deceitful. Next day, we called him and there was a message on the answer-phone saying he, too, had left. For all we knew, Clem was now the only company man left in Kuwait.

66

We promptly began hatching our own escape plans. If they could do it, it was still not too late. We needed a four-wheel-drive and a bedouin to guide us around the Iraqi troop positions in the desert. A guide could be hired for about $180 and the motor dealers, Al Ghanim, were selling their jeeps on credit. The only other possibility was by camel!

Just as we began making inquiries, the BBC announced that a Briton had been shot dead while trying to escape to Saudi Arabia. It was widely publicised in the West, and British Embassy people twice tried to recover his body but, as far as I know, it was never found. The incident caused us to abandon all thoughts of escape. We soon had cause to regret we did not take the risk.

August 17 was one of the most fateful days of all for Westerners. The entire community was seized by confusion and fear when both BBC and Voice of America reported an Iraqi order that we should all turn ourselves in. The Americans were told to report to the International, and the Britons to the Regency Palace. They were two of the city's most luxurious hotels and both were situated on the seaside road, though 20 kilometres apart. A call from the US Embassy at about 3 p.m. confirmed the report and told Clem and Ski to move to the International before dusk. It was, they said, an Iraqi order to ensure the safety of American citizens.

We didn't know what to make of it. Was this an arrest order, or preparations for the evacuation? Should Ikuko and I go too, or would they separate us from the men? The embassy could not say. We began packing. We had less than two hours to get there. But even as we packed, we were debating whether to comply. As the embassy had urged us to go, perhaps we should. They wouldn't throw us to the lions, surely? There was also the fact that

I was not American and I did not particularly want to walk straight into Iraqi hands. I decided to wait to see what the British were recommending.

I called Richard Hattersley, my local warden. He and Sandy Macmillan, the warden in the Salwa district where our flat was, would prove to be among the most cool-headed, reliable and helpful people I met during the entire crisis. It was only the second time I had spoken to Richard. 'Stay put for an hour or two until we get some more information,' he advised. Randy Taylor, an American we had befriended on the phone, said he was going, but he had heard that a long queue had formed at the hotel and he had decided to wait for a while. Bill Van Rye was not sure what to do and he too decided to wait at home. The BBC news contained a Foreign Office announcement relaying the Iraqi order that Britons should report to the Regency Palace. Having been at odds with the State Department on day one over what their nationals should do, Britain was now lined up closely with the US in giving similarly dubious advice.

'Those who wish to go to the hotel should take their own food and one suitcase,' the announcement said.

'What on earth do they mean by "those who wish",' I was shouting. I was furious. 'It is not what I wish. The question is, what is the safest thing to do? I want them to tell me what's *safe* for me to do!'

Richard had made up his mind. 'I'm not going anywhere, nor are any other Brits I know,' he said. 'If your friends [Clem and Ski] insist on going, you are welcome to stay with us.'

The phone calls rained in, with most people saying they, too, would refuse to go. By the time William Walde-grave, the British Foreign Office Minister, had described the Iraqi order as 'a sinister move which would lead to the internment of British nationals', scores of Britons had already gone to the hotel, only to be turned away by puzzled hotel staff. We never did discover what went wrong and why the Iraqis were not waiting to receive their 'guests'.

This was not the end of our worries. The Iraqis had warned that those failing to comply would face 'unspecified difficulties'. It sounded like a veiled threat. We were afraid there would be a house-to-house search that very night. We thought it was time to move again. Ikuko called Hirohiso Shirai, a young Japanese Embassy official. I had met Shirai, who had become a friend of my teenage niece Breda when she visited Kuwait the previous summer. (Breda was to have returned to Kuwait on August 6 and Shirai would have met her at the airport. Fortunately, the invasion pre-empted the visit; if it hadn't, I would have had an extra responsibility and would have been sick with worry about her safety.)

Since the invasion Shirai had moved into the embassy and was only too happy to give us the keys to his flat. His Kuwaiti landlord put the damper on that idea; he was too afraid. The Iraqis had threatened to blow up the homes of any Kuwaitis found sheltering Westerners. We had no choice but to stay put. I was concerned that we might be picked up at any time and when I finally got to sleep that night I wondered whether I would wake up in the same bed next morning.

IX

We stayed where we were and, despite our forebodings, it was a peaceful night and the morning began much as had become normal. We had coffee but after chatting over breakfast, we suddenly decided to leave Ski's flat. On the face of it, it was a spontaneous decision, but it was really the result of a growing tension among the four of us. We were all strong personalities, cooped up in a small one-bedroomed flat. Ski and Ikuko were perfect hosts. And that was part of the problem. They treated us as favoured guests. They surrendered their bedroom while they slept in the sitting room; he on a sofa, she on two armchairs joined together. It was an arrangement that made me feel uneasy but they wouldn't have it any other way. We tried to do our bit about the flat and help with some of the meals. I washed the dishes and Clem cooked a few times, but it was Ikuko's kitchen and she did the vast bulk of the work. When we first arrived the atmosphere was wonderful. We all sat discussing the stories we had heard, and what had happened to us since the invasion, and our prospects for the future. We were convinced the Americans would come, but when? It was the honeymoon period and we all seemed well-suited. But, I became increasingly aware, and with some discomfort, that Clem was taking over. He spoke too loudly and, gesticulating airily, I thought he tended to dominate most conversations. Almost silent in our flat, he now seemed to me to go to the other extreme.

Clem is an exuberant and forceful personality. His military training had reinforced these tendencies and now, as an educator, he was used to lecturing and taking charge. I was afraid others might regard him as intimidating and resent it. But nobody seemed to mind and I relaxed. We were relieved to have been given refuge, and Ikuko and Ski were glad that they could help. But I knew we would have to adapt to the new situation. I was quite enthusiastic about it. I liked the idea of a communal life and, in this case, the Japanese flavour to our daily routine. I had been to Japan and had a close friend there. Listening to Ikuko speak on the phone brought back happy memories.

Ikuko, petite with shining long hair, looked much younger than her forty-five years. She managed to be assertive yet gentle at the same time. I liked that in her. I knew Ski only slightly more. Having worked with him I knew he was a man of high principle, and that commitment was the most important word in his vocabulary. I had found it hard to share his commitment to the newspaper. It was always an uphill struggle, especially since censorship had been introduced when the National Assembly was dissolved in 1986. Our material was not only heavily censored but it was difficult enough gathering information in the first place. Compared with other Western expatriates we were appallingly paid. I was among the best paid and I earned the equivalent of $18,000 a year. Clem earned perhaps five times as much, with all kinds of other perks thrown in. But these niggling problems and my inability to share Ski's commitment seemed trivial and a long way behind us now. Living with Ski and his wife, I was eager to fit in with their lifestyle and cause them a minimum of disruption.

There was one underlying and recurring worry. My relationship with Clem was troubling me. We disagreed about almost everything. He became annoyed if I contradicted him in front of other people. These differences

71

were nothing new, and I remembered the rows we used to have back at our flat. But then we had privacy and now we were not at home. What made it worse was that Clem seemed not to notice. What really got me down was that he never seemed to stop talking, and had an opinion on absolutely everything. He might have thought he was keeping our spirits up. It was not so much what he said that I objected to; he is an articulate, intelligent man. But I thought he too often sounded dogmatic and insensitive to others, and his six-foot and heavy build tended to make him seem intimidating. I would scan the faces of Ski and Ikuko for their reaction, but they were too polite to say anything, though I could detect a hint of frustration, and on a couple of occasions I distinctly sensed it.

One night Clem wanted to watch a video. Ikuko was still in the kitchen, clearing up after dinner.

'Let's watch a movie,' Clem said.

'Let's wait for Iko-Chan,' Ski replied.

Clem began calling her and urging her to hurry up. I thought that she might be too tired, or might not want to watch a film.

We were also sitting in what had become their bedroom.

On another occasion, Ikuko showed she was vexed by Clem's insistent questions. He became upset when he discovered Ikuko and I had paid $36 for a new gas cooking cylinder which was twenty times the price before the invasion. We had done it to avoid the risk of standing in a queue in the heat and perhaps being seen by the Iraqis. There were also signs that the Kuwaiti money we were using would soon become worthless. Clem was by no means a miserly man but in this case he insisted we had been cheated. We knew we had, too, but this, we told him, was war. He went on for what seemed an inordinate length of time. When I tried to change the subject he wouldn't let it drop. He turned on Ikuko and fired off one question after another. I cringed with embarrassment, and she began struggling with her English, until finally she turned to Ski in desperation and pleaded: 'Please, Oto-san, explain to him.'

Clem even gave them advice on what they should pack in the event of an evacuation. I was afraid it could wreck our relationship with them. One morning, I felt it was already beyond repair. For some days Ski had looked taut, and depressed. He said little, while Clem continued, seemingly unaware of the situation. There was nothing I felt I could do. But this couldn't go on.

Clem phoned our neighbours in Salwa. They said all was quiet. 'Let's go home,' he said. Within an hour we had made our explanations and were back in our flat. Ski and Ikuko must have been glad to see us go; they did not protest.

It was good to be home again. And to be alone, if only to conduct our rows in private. Our privacy, however, was to be short-lived. Our own guests were already on their way.

X

We seemed to be under constant threat, but of course we weren't. People were being picked up. Several groups of Westerners who made a dash for the Saudi border ran into Iraqi patrols and ended up as hostages at the Regency Palace. Others were being taken away at roadblocks. We were lucky in that, on our few trips out, we had avoided checkpoints. The Iraqis were still in the process of establishing control and there were long stretches of highways with no blocks. Some people were being turned in by Arab neighbours or thieves. We knew the threat existed, but it was absurd to believe that the whole Iraqi Army was searching for us. It was not knowing if and, more importantly, when they might come that nourished my fears. The uncertainty was always with us.

It was during the third week of August, after the initial series of shocks we had absorbed in the wake of the invasion, that a pattern began to emerge in our lives. It began with the news, or a rumour, of a new arrest, another Iraqi raid, a new punitive law, a reported evacuation, or a shoot-out in the neighbourhood. Angry and frightened, we would instinctively run for cover. When the danger subsided, we would raise our heads and start moving around again, turning up the volume on the radio and TV and switching on a few lights after dark. At times we even ventured on to the roof for a spot of sun or just to look around, though still stooping to avoid being seen by the soldiers stationed on the balcony beneath the dome of the mosque on the seafront. This would go on until another alarm was raised.

This pattern of ups and downs continued until the end of the war. Sometimes triggered by an upsurge of Iraqi activity, it was also a product of our siege mentality. It was best illustrated in the number and variety of stories that found their way around the network of those who had gone to ground. Many of the tales were quite frightening, though how true we never knew. We heard that Iraqi civilians, entire families, were coming to Kuwait and evicting people from their own homes so that they could move in. Looting was rampant. Iraqi soldiers and civilians, and an assortment of Arabs, were breaking into flats, stopping people in the streets and taking their cars, snatching gold chains from the necks of Indian women. Groups of black labourers descended on the city and only later did we find out that they were Sudanese workers. The Iraqis had brought them in to help them load the stolen goods on to trucks bound for Iraq. In the meantime, we heard that the first Kuwaiti dead were being taken to the Mubarak Hospital, many with bullet holes in their heads.

The cycle in this pattern was sometimes disconcertingly short. The day we returned home from Jabriya our spirits were lifted by the uneventful drive and the semblance of normality surrounding our apartment block. We relaxed and I thought: 'It's not so bad, it could be worse.' We were so at ease that we decided to visit Nirmala for lunch at her flat in Sha'ab up the coast road towards the city. As we were about to leave, Sheila called. According to the US Embassy, she said, the Iraqis had received orders to shoot foreigners on sight. We were immediately plunged back into the abyss. We cancelled the lunch and phoned Ski. He called someone else and the upshot was that the Iraqis would shoot only those trying to escape across the border. Randy Taylor said the Americans had been advised to stay indoors, which was the same advice that Britons had been given from the beginning.

Bill Van Rye spoke of house-to-house searches and these were confirmed by the BBC reporting that at least eight Britons and eight Frenchmen had been taken from their homes with only a case. We leapt into action, first removing the batteries from the clock to stop it from chiming. We also moved my computer and our video camera to the home of Omar's father along the road. Bill told us not to answer the door if the Iraqis came. They were not, he said, breaking down the doors. For hours we stayed virtually silent, just watching and listening, but nobody came.

On August 20, my father's seventy-fourth birthday, I got a call from the Yugoslav Embassy. They were preparing an official evacuation in a convoy led by a Yugoslav diplomat. Clem urged me to go. So did my friends. They almost convinced me of its good sense, but deep down I had no desire to leave Kuwait. I was already accustomed to this new strange way of life and was beginning to feel a sense of Ski's commitment. For the first time, perhaps, in my five years in Kuwait I felt I almost belonged here. But I needed to find something to provide me with a more tangible reason to stay, and also to convince the others.

The opportunity was presented by Nirmala. She told me the Iraqis were checking car registration documents at the Iraqi border. The Iraqis were also turning back those with passports issued after the invasion. Good. I now could not travel in my own car, because my registration book said I was British and my Yugoslav passport had been issued only on August 11. I called Demirok for advice. As a diplomat, I thought he was in a better position to know. But he was either unwilling or unable to give advice directly.

When I asked him if I should leave, he answered ambiguously: 'I am not going.'

I was anxious for him to assess the danger to me. But it was unfair; I was asking him to make my decision for me. Instead he said, if I could cope with food shortages, I should be all right. This was sufficient for me, the die was cast. I was definitely not going.

I wrote an affectionate letter to my father. It was the only birthday present I could give him. I wrote another one to my mother in which I tried neither to dramatise nor to underplay my situation.

I had to deliver my letters to the embassy before 7 a.m. because the convoy was to leave at 7.30. Anxious to avoid the checkpoint at the Messilah intersection, instead of turning left from our building to the Gulf road I turned right, driving through small alleyways and over waste-land to a dual carriageway leading on to the Fahaheel expressway. Just as I turned the corner on to the dual carriageway, I saw a truck full of soldiers ahead of me. I balked at the sight and stepped on the brake. There were no other cars in the road. I saw the truck making a U-turn and going the way I was supposed to take. My first instinct was just to drive past the U-turn to avoid the truck. But I changed my mind. I knew that sooner or later I would have to face the Iraqis. I drove slowly behind the truck. The soldiers were peering at me curiously. We were now on the narrow approach road to the expressway and I could not overtake the truck. But then it slowed down and the driver put his arm out of the window, motioning me to pass him. He pulled to the right making way for me. I stepped on the accelerator and as I passed him I waved a thank you to the driver. He smiled back.

The embassy was in the middle of the city and as I drove on towards the Maghreb motorway, I saw a number of checkpoints along the motorway. I began feeling nervous. It was too late to turn back, I was on the one-way approach road. The Iraqis had erected blocks every 200 metres. They used metal barriers which they placed on both sides of the road, but with a space between them, so that a car had to stop or at least slow down to squeeze round them. A couple of soldiers were standing at the first barrier. There were several others standing by the roadside. They were all armed with rifles. At the first checkpoint there was a queue of cars. Some were being asked to pull up by the roadside while their cars were inspected. Others were just waved straight through.

I kept my fingers crossed. When my turn came a soldier stopped me and asked in Arabic for my documents. He looked at me closely and obviously recognised me as a foreigner. I gave him my passport but he had trouble reading it; there was nothing in Arabic inside. He asked me to pull over and pointed to where I should stop. I thought: 'This is it.' This was my first face-to-face contact with an Iraqi soldier and he was unsmiling. He asked me to open the boot. I got out and opened it. He looked inside and felt around with his hands, no doubt looking for weapons. He went to the front passenger seat and felt under it, and also opened the glove compartment. He then indicated with his head I could go. I had been standing by the car while he inspected it and by this time my shirt was soaked with sweat from the heat and fright. I was waved through all the other checkpoints and when I arrived at the embassy safely, I felt like a veteran. I had had my first major test and come through it. I felt quite proud.

At the embassy I gave the letters for my parents to a Yugoslav engineer. I hugged and kissed goodbye the people I knew, among them Sheila, who had decided to leave with her son. Michael was staying behind. When the column of cars, loaded to the brink with people and possessions, began moving, I suddenly felt the tears well up again. I could imagine my parents' distress when they found I was not among the convoy when it got to Belgrade. As it turned out, it was my sister Vanja who was waiting at Belgrade Airport. She later told me of her wait for the refugee flight. She wrote on a placard: 'Do you have any information about Jadranka Porter?'

'I never thought I would have to do something like that. This was the kind of stuff I saw people do in the movies,' she told me later. She was even more worried no one came forward with information about me. She is not a religious person, but on this occasion she asked her Egyptian boyfriend to go to the mosque and pray for my safety.

As I stood alone on the pavement waving goodbye to the last of the evacuees, I thought, there goes my last chance of escape.

XI

The invasion caught us with our food stocks down. That was largely my fault. Clem was a compulsive buyer and he had access to the stores at the Al Jaber military base where food was available at subsidised prices. Our home had always been well-stocked, but Clem had been back in the country only two days when the invasion took place. At first, food was the last thing on my mind. I was too excited by what was going on around me. While I was busy gathering information on the phone, my friends were going from one shop to another, emptying the shelves. I thought the concern about food was exaggerated, anyway. When I went to the Sultan Centre in Salwa on my way home from the newspaper to collect my passport, I just bought my usual basketful. But as soon as we went into hiding, food loomed large as a potentially enormous problem. This was not only because of the shortages and our inability to go out. We had endless disagreements over what our needs were and what our consumption should be.

In the beginning, we relied on food brought to us by Nirmala and our Palestinian neighbours. We also remembered dozens of cans of vegetables, hotdogs and fish Clem had bought a long time before but which we had never used. We ate the perishable stuff and kept the cans for later. In this way we managed to build up quite a neat little stockpile. When we went to stay with Sheila, we took the food with us and by the time we returned two weeks later, we realised our supplies had fallen dramati-

80

cally. Some of it had been eaten, but some of it had just got lost in the moves. Our departure from Sheila's and Ski's had been so sudden, the last thing to concern us was whether we had all our food with us. And in any case, you just don't raid other people's fridges, taking what's yours.

So on the evening of our return from Ski's, we had our poorest meal for a long time: corned beef and biscuits. But it was also the one we most relished. We had plenty of homemade wine and we mixed it with lemonade and made Wine Coolers. So good did that meal taste that it was then I realised I could survive on almost anything, and, if need be, I would share my last morsel. That need never arose and Kuwait never ran out of basic food items. At the time of the invasion it was common knowledge there was enough food to last the 1.8 million people six months. Over the next few months people were leaving at such a rate that by the end of the war there were barely 400,000 left in the country, excluding the Iraqi forces, though, for them, food was near the top of their looting list. Even Clem, who hated my going out, agreed it was necessary to scout for food.

The main food stores in Kuwait were the Co-operatives and these were reasonably well-stocked and the most obvious target for shoppers. Not for me. To get through the doors you had to show a Kuwaiti identity card, mainly to ensure that people shopped in their own areas and didn't stockpile by going from one Co-op to another. My ID showed I was British and I was afraid of being turned in to the Iraqis.

One day in August I went to Salmiya, a popular centre about 15 kilometres from the city. It was mainly inhabited by foreigners, though it was also a favourite place for Kuwaiti shoppers. I knew it well, having lived there for four years. At the Salmiya Co-op I found a

81

queue about 60 metres long. They were mainly Arabs with their Indian and Filipino maids, all standing three abreast. An armed and helmeted soldier was there to maintain order. It was about 8.30 in the morning and the Co-op had not yet opened, so I drove away, hoping to get what I needed in one of the bakalas, the small corner grocery shops. There were scores of them dotted around Salmiya, but they had mostly been emptied of all their foodstuffs. In one, I found some onions, in another, some milk and two bottles of mineral water, in a third I bought twenty eggs. It was a far cry from the days when one of the favourite pastimes in Kuwait had been shopping.

When I arrived at the roundabout linking Al Khansa and Al Bahrain Street, I saw a teenage boy hawker, a Palestinian, I think, standing beside a pile of eggs, onions and potatoes. I bought as much of each as I could carry for KD 10 ($36). This was expensive by old standards but this was for survival and could keep us going for quite a while, if it came to the crunch.

I drove along Al Bahrain Street, towards the seafront, in my hunt for more. As I approached the Gulf coast road, I saw an army patrol and took a fast right-turn. It was lucky. On the left I spotted a bakala with a nylon sheet for a door. When I walked in, my eyes popped. There was everything: bread, milk, bananas, apples, cans of soft drinks, tinned meat, coffee. The prices were high but I was so relieved I was ready to pay anything. The owner, a Jordanian, was charming. He helped me choose and I loaded the car to the limit and left for home. I felt a great sense of achievement.

The next day, despite Clem's complaints about my taking unnecessary risks, I returned to find an Iraqi soldier sitting on a chair in front of the shop. I carried on driving for about 20 or 30 metres, then stopped and beckoned a passerby, an Egyptian. I asked him to ask in the shop if it were safe for me to go in. He went and reappeared, nodding his head. This time it was full of people, and I sensed the tension caused by my presence. I could hear Kuwaitis asking the owner in low voices whether I was 'Inglesia'. Then a shot rang out and I jumped. Everyone else went about their business as if nothing had happened. I lowered my head and did my shopping fast. Outside, a bystander told me a soldier had just fired in the air for no apparent reason. The Iraqis were getting restive. I drove away and never returned to that shop. Whenever I passed it, there were always too many soldiers around for my liking.

I hid the food all over the flat as a precaution against thieves. We kept the bulk of it in the kitchen but I also put jars, cans, and bags of flour and rice in the bedroom wardrobe, on shelves behind the books, in chests of drawers with the underwear and socks.

When we left Sheila's, Sameer volunteered to take care of our food needs, but now Sheila had called to say that he was afraid to go out with his catering van. He had already had one confiscated by the Iraqis in our area. Salah, however, was not deterred. He came with a Filipino masseuse and two poodles, one of which did its business on our carpet. Salah said he had enough food to last him a year, and then handed us a box containing fewer than a dozen items. But you don't look a gift horse in the mouth.

Clem was in charge of cooking. He favoured rich and spicy meals and I noticed that our stock of some items, such as oil, was fast diminishing. I spoke to him about it, but he brushed my concern aside. It was insignificant, he said.

In late August, on the advice of our neighbours, I stopped going out to shop for food. They said it was too risky and were afraid the Iraqis would follow me back to the apartment block. Instead, they offered to do the shopping for us. I had no choice but to agree. We also heard, from an American, that food could be delivered to our home. The Americans had organised a supply network using Arabs to do the shopping and the delivery. I thought it could only be a good idea to diversify our sources of supply.

That was the end of my food worries. From then on, until the hostages left Kuwait, I became part of a food delivery network for those in hiding.

XII

We had barely settled in after returning from Ski's place when Omar called, asking if we could give shelter to an American couple.

'Sure, when are they coming?' said Clem.

'Now. They're already here.'

Naomi Charchalis wore a hejab, the Arab headscarf, and abaya, a black chador covering her from head to toe. George, her husband, was in a green tracksuit. They looked hot, flustered and frightened. They had just been evicted by a Kuwaiti from a villa he had put at their disposal after they fled their apartment. Their block had been in full view of the troops on the beach and soldiers had walked in and out at will. The Kuwaiti had got cold feet after the Iraqis threatened to blow up houses sheltering Westerners. Many Kuwaitis ignored the threat, including one middle-aged Kuwaiti woman I knew. She gave refuge to an American for months until all Westerners were allowed to leave in December.

George was Omar's boss. He had been working on a project to 'green' Kuwait and he was an erudite, articulate, urbane man of sixty, well-read and widely travelled. He appreciated the quality things of life. Back in the States he had mixed with prominent businessmen and had friends among senators. He was also something of a dandy. He wore handmade shirts and owned an overcoat modelled on one worn by Marlon Brando in the *Godfather* movie. Noticing such ephemera was a sign of our pre-occupation with the minutiae of life while living so closely to each other. After they left Kuwait with only a small bag, I managed to save their luggage, which contained much of George's wardrobe, from looters.

Naomi, or Nome, as we called her, was a handsome woman even now, in her late fifties, and with only a few possessions with her, she still managed to look smart. The world was a simple place to Nome. There were good people and bad people. Saddam was a brute and our situation was a 'sticky wicket', a phrase she must have picked up from her English friends: she didn't seem the type to watch cricket.

'And what is your opinion of the latest situation?' George asked Clem soon after they had arrived. He spoke in a formal, measured monotone, choosing his words carefully. Boy! I thought to myself, more amused than worried; we are now going to sit here the whole afternoon. But by then I had stopped worrying about the impression Clem and I made on other people. We were in our own home, on our own ground. We would do what we could to make them comfortable, but they would have to take us as they found us. George's opening question and the prospects for our release were thrashed out daily until we parted company. George was as eager to talk as Clem, though less demonstrative and excitable. When there seemed no more to say they began all over again.

George and Nome were fed up. They listened to me talk enthusiastically about events and encouraged me to write. But they did not share my excitement. 'I'm too tired to get excited about this,' said Nome. 'I need comfort, not adventure.' George and Clem expected an American attack in late August. By now the core of the alliance against Iraq had been formed and allied troops and weaponry were already arriving in Saudi Arabia, supposedly to defend the Saudis. We were convinced they were massing for the liberation of Kuwait.

Clem and George felt the refusal of Western embassies to close, and of diplomats to leave by the August 24 deadline ordered by Baghdad, would spark off an incident that would serve as a pretext for an allied offensive. When it didn't happen, George was crestfallen. Pyschologically, it seemed to have become necessary for him to set another deadline as a way of coping. While giving the allies another two weeks to prepare for war, he was giving himself fourteen more days of hope.

I sympathised with him. All of us were in a similar frame of mind. We could not forget we were prisoners. At night we lived in darkness and never turned the light on in the rooms facing the street. Then it turned out the hours in darkness were not safe either. The Iraqis had been looking for abandoned homes and emptying them of their contents. So we were advised to keep a discreet light on, lest we attracted the soldier-thieves. Each time the doorbell rang we stiffened. We were also worried when the phone rang and there was a silence, or a thick Arabic accent, at the other end of the line. It could be an Iraqi checking for Westerners. Most of all, we felt hemmed in by the troops all around us. They were on the main road and occupied a house close by. A night patrol was also using a prefabricated cabin in a street behind ours. Army trucks began using our once quiet little road. We couldn't even take out garbage in case we bumped into soldiers. Our Palestinian neighbours helped us enormously and served as a screen to cover our presence. We felt we were in the middle of a hornet's nest. There were, though, some advantages in our isolation. The fact we were surrounded by troops, we reasoned, should mean we were safe from marauders; so long as we stayed 'invisible'.

Adding to our concern were our suspicions about a couple of people, non-Westerners, we were in touch with on the telephone. They would call us each time the news spread about fresh detentions of Westerners. They said they were checking to make sure we were all right, but they also seemed unusually interested in what was happening to our cars and other possessions. One offered to look after our flat if we were arrested. We felt there was an ulterior motive behind their undue concern for our well-being. Those were the days when new entrepreneurs were springing up, selling cars, TVs and furniture from houses whose occupants had fled. Such things fetched high prices from Iraqi civilians who had followed in the wake of the invading troops, and had cash but nothing to buy with it back in Iraq. We weren't suspicious of friends but of others who surfaced during the occupation with offers of help, with forged documents, food, or suggestions for a new escape route to Saudi Arabia. Our fears were probably unjustified, but at the time, and throughout the occupation, trust was an elusive quality and in short supply. Our main worry was that we would be turned in.

George, meanwhile, began growing a beard and ate very little. He said he was on a diet, although he was already as thin as a rake. A swift and decisive American attack on Iraq would have been a cure for all his worries.

'They should just get in there and squash Saddam like a damn bug,' George raged. We all spoke of the early days of the invasion when hopes of an attack were much higher.

'We thought we would wake up one morning and see the USS Eisenhower sitting in the Gulf,' said George.

'Where is it, George, where is it?' asked Nome, as if he had promised her a gift and failed to deliver.

'If only we had that damn Pajero [four-wheel-drive] we could have got out,' said George.

'Well, we don't have it. We haven't gotten out and we are stuck,' shot back Nome. That put an end to George's reveries.

We shared many poignant moments with George and Nome during their stay with us. I remember how our hearts went out to the Irish hostage when he was released in Beirut and spoke about his captivity. We found inspiration from an unexpected quarter. An American pilot, who broadcast to all hostages in the Middle East over Voice of America, spoke of his seven years as a prisoner of war in Vietnam.

'No matter how much you hurt,' he said, 'you should try to help others. Take one day at a time and have faith in yourself and your government.'

This was about the most valuable piece of advice we had throughout the occupation. Trying to help others would bring a sense of purpose into my life and reduce the anguish when I found myself alone.

We were all heartened and angered, too, by news of escape. The AT & T (American Telephone and Telegraph) Company had managed to get several dozen of its people out of Kuwait in the first two weeks after the invasion. We were happy for those who escaped, but furious that a private company had been better prepared than the US Embassy or State Department. An AT & T manager described over Voice of America how their crisis management centre sprang into action, plotting escape routes with the help of their staff in Riyadh and Kuwait before the telephone lines were cut. Asked whether the company had any help from the State Department the man said: 'I am not aware of the details of their plan and am not able to compare the AT & T crisis centre with theirs.' We would have been surprised if the State Department had even thought of a crisis plan.

George, Nome and Clem were bitter that, instead of being with their families in the States, they were listening to nightly gun battles between resistance fighters and Iraqi patrols. The Iraqi crackdown was getting harsher. In a letter I wrote on September 12 I said: 'The situation has taken a turn for the worse. The Iraqis have announced harsh measures, escalating their reign of terror. As we watch, confusion gradually gives place to more organised looting, hunting down of innocent people and killing. We shudder at the thought of what might come next. The crackdown follows what sounded like heavy gunfire or a series of large explosions on two consecutive nights, last Monday and Tuesday. There is little doubt that the firing was related to the activities of the Kuwaiti resistance fighters who are regularly involved in skirmishes with the Iraqis. They are paying with their lives for their nightly sorties.' The Iraqis had begun by blowing up houses used by Kuwaiti snipers for attacks on troops. Now, the resistance moved in to unfinished houses, whose construction had been halted by the invasion. There were a number of unfinished villas in our area and every so often we could hear short but fierce gunfights taking place close to our home. On these occasions, we kept away from the windows for fear of stray bullets. When the fighting died down, we would wait fearfully to see whether the Iraqis came to search for Kuwaitis and weapons. Luckily, they never did.

At midnight on September 2, exactly a month after the invasion, there was a sudden rooftop uproar. The Kuwaitis went out in their masses on to the roofs and for an hour shouted 'Alahu Akbar' (God is Great) into the night. It was an awesome chant and seemed to symbolise all our despair. It was a cry for help, but also an act of defiance against the invaders. I was a bundle of emotions and shivered as each new wave of prayers rolled across the rooftops. I ran to the bathroom and listened through the fan, then into the bedroom. I opened a window a crack when suddenly a massive fusillade of shots went off, as if hundreds of guns had been fired simultaneously. My heart sank. I imagined scores of bodies falling in mid-prayer. But the shouts of Alahu Akbar continued. I could even distinguish voices, men's and women's, hoarse and breathless, as if in a trance. The next day I learnt that the Iraqis had fired into the air to try to quieten the crowds and no one had been hurt.

September 9 was a very special day. It was to George and Nome that I ran, elated, after Clem and I had heard on the BBC's British Press Review that my first letter to Alan Brown, my friend in England, had been published in the *Sunday Times*. I was ecstatic. It was one of the most prestigious newspapers in the world and I was in it. The news was fantastic encouragement, and stayed so until the end of the war. The BBC said the story was based on a letter written by a woman journalist and smuggled out of Kuwait by a Yugoslav diplomat. This meant my letters to my parents must have reached them. I was so relieved. I had done my duty to my parents and my profession. It was the best feeling so far.

It was while George and Nome were with us that we began to limit our phone calls to two minutes each, as a safety measure. It was Clem's idea, but also widely prac-tised by others, particularly among Americans, many of whom even spoke in code. For example, when they wanted to give a telephone number they would say some-thing like: 'The first digit is the same as in your number, the second is double that, the third is the number of players in tennis doubles' and so on. Another American friend, George Daher, would not answer his phone unless I made two calls, allowing it to ring three times with a two-minute pause between calls. But my British and Indian friends scoffed at such precautions. If the Iraqis wanted to trace us, there were easier ways than bugging our calls. I never suspected the phone might be our undoing and did not strictly apply the two-minute rule, though I did warn callers about it. It became the cause of a big row with Clem.

One morning Zeinab, my Indian friend, phoned. I mentioned the two-minute limit but she was too anxious to tell me what had happened. Dozens of soldiers had just swooped on her house in Suleibikhat, entering through the front door, the sitting-room window, the kitchen door and the roof. She described it at length and I noticed Clem shifting nervously on the bed. Then he began to mutter. Two minutes was by no means enough for Zeinab's story. 'Zeinab, just a minute, Zeinab,' I tried to stop her, but she went on. Clem suddenly turned over, hit the receiver rest with his hand and disconnected the line. I was furious. I felt a rush of anger and I spat fire. He walked out and returned to say he had called a meeting in the kitchen. The three of them were sitting round the table. It was an inquest. This was stupid, I thought; I couldn't believe it.

I sat down. In a solemn voice Clem opened the proceedings. 'Jadranka is putting all our lives in danger,' he said. 'We have to stop her. In fact, if anyone here speaks on the phone for more than two minutes it is the duty of the others to stop them.'

I was appalled. At worst, he was treating me as if I were on trial, with him the prosecutor. At best, I was an errant schoolgirl. I guessed what he was doing. Having failed to handle me on his own, he was dragging in George and Nome. He knew they would not contradict him, because this was his flat. But it was mine, too. I was paying part of the rent, but you would never have guessed it from Clem's behaviour. George said he was trying to keep his calls short, and that he was sure I was not deliberately doing anything to endanger our safety. But Clem added insult to injury. I was to promise, in front of all, that I would abide by the rules. I hated him. I wanted to punch him in the face. Instead I sat silently and began to cry. They were more tears of anger than sorrow. I was so angry I thought if I were to put a match to my tears they would burst into flames. I refused to speak.

Then Clem dropped a bombshell. 'When I objected to Jadranka's long calls she told me to fuck off,' he said. It was true, but for him to repeat it was hitting below the belt. George and Nome never swore. The only expletive ever to pass their lips was 'damn'. There was, I thought, no cause for involving them in our fights. Anyway, they knew we were at loggerheads without us having to tell them. If they were surprised they didn't show it, but there was an uncomfortable silence. It was all turning nasty. I was getting tired of it; I wanted it finished.

'I have no intention of hurting anyone,' I said, which was true, and I promised to stick to the two-minute limit. Then I got up and left the kitchen.

I knew this was the end. There was nothing that would keep Clem and me permanently together. But I would stick it out until the crisis was over.

Later that afternoon, George showed me some sympathy. 'Poor old Clem, he does go on a bit, doesn't he?' he said.

Three or four days later, Nome put her name on the list for evacuation after Saddam Hussein announced all women and children were to be set free. Saddam's decision was a relief for hundreds of wives and children, but it made him no more popular in Kuwait than in Britain or America. We saw the TV film of Saddam with British families in a staged performance designed to show

93

his humanity. We were as revolted at the sight of his ruffling that little boy's hair as everyone else was. If anything, we felt even worse. Their humiliation in front of the cameras was the crowning insult after what they had suffered in captivity in the weeks after the invasion. Like us, they had lived in fear and dread, not knowing what to do next. For those with children, wondering if they might ever be separated, it was heartbreaking.

I had already declined a seat on the bus that had carried British women to Baghdad a few days earlier. It was the first of a series of evacuations which ran anything but smoothly. Some sixty British women were detained at checkpoints on their way to the assembly point and finally arrived in Baghdad two days later. More frightening was the fact that while Baghdad was releasing women and children, it was making up the numbers of captives by detaining more men. On September 5, sixteen Western men were picked up. They were arrested after a Frenchman was detained at a checkpoint and asked to go home to collect his belongings. The Iraqis took his luggage and discovered fourteen Britons and a German hiding in the apartment block where he lived.

It did not take long for Nome to decide to leave; though it wasn't an easy decision for her to take. She and George had been married for more than thirty years and, although they had been separated before by George's work, the last thing she wanted to do was leave him. But she was anxious to see their daughters, Camille and Alexandra, back in the United States. She was also tired of the captivity and what they saw as America's foot-dragging in not coming to Kuwait's aid. While she was grateful for what we had done for them, she was not comfortable. She wanted to be in her own home and she said as much. I understood.

There was a danger the Iraqis might question wives

and force them to reveal the whereabouts of their husbands. So Nome prepared a story. She would say George was Greek, which in fact was his origin, and he was out of the country at the time of the invasion. There was also the problem of transport to the airport. Only the first British evacuees left Kuwait by bus; all subsequent evacuations, British, American and French, were by plane. The Embassy had stressed that on no account was her husband to drive her. We thought of one of the cabs still operating, but Clem was afraid the driver might turn us in. I was ready to drive her myself, but no one else relished the idea. In the end, one of their Palestinian friends obliged.

When he came next morning, Nome was not ready. She had been violently sick throughout the night. We thought it was nerves. We were all concerned. George tried to put on a brave front, but I thought he, too, was reaching the end of his tether. There was nothing we could do. Nome finally left Kuwait a week later. From the radio and television news we learned that she was well on the road to safety.

On the same day I wrote in my letter: 'They are combing through the area I live in. The Arabs sheltering Westerners have so far managed to keep the soldiers from entering the buildings. But don't let that be published in case it reaches the Iraqis and they become more thorough and aggressive.' It was not published, but it made no difference. Two days later our luck ran out.

XIII

The doctor, alias Salah, the caterer — whom we had last seen the day we left Sheila's — began to keep in constant touch. He phoned and called regularly and seemed always eager to help. Within a week of our return to Salwa, Salah began urging us to move. He had just the flat for us in Reggai, a comparatively new neighbourhood, about 25 kilometres away. But we had had quite enough of moving. We didn't want to leave our flat or lose our independence, and besides, there was nothing to suggest that Salwa, despite the heavy concentration of troops on the seafront, was any more dangerous than Reggai or anywhere else, for that matter. We were familiar with the goings on around us, we had monitored the troop movements, and we did not like the idea of having to get used to another flat in another place which was a less known quantity.

'What about your car?' Salah asked one day. The Iraqis were confiscating cars from anyone unable to prove their ownership. We had heard about some people who had been detained for theft while driving cars belonging to their relatives. Clem's was a rented car and not registered in his name. We gave Salah the registration book and he promised to fix it. We never saw the book again. Then he told us the Iraqis were monitoring telephone calls and the cordless ones were much easier to tap. We had a cordless phone, so Clem replaced it with an ordinary one. Next time he came, Salah asked if he could borrow our cordless one for a week. We never saw that again either.

Our suspicions of Salah were growing by the day. On one visit he ran his eyes hungrily over the shelves on which the TV, video recorder and hi-fi system stood. Then I noticed his eyes lingering on my hands. I felt distinctly uneasy. I rarely wear jewellery, apart from two silver rings, and my watch was only of the plastic Swatch variety. But it was common knowledge in Kuwait that every woman kept jewellery somewhere. Salah gave the impression that every time his eyes rested on one of our possessions, he was mentally converting it into cash.

The alarm bells finally rang. I wanted to stop our relationship with Salah. But how were we to call a halt to his visits and phone calls without arousing his suspicions and resentment? It could, we thought, cost us dearly if he decided to be difficult. We had no idea who he knew or what might happen if he turned nasty. So we kept up the pretence, chatting as casually as possible to conceal our concern.

Our anxiety mounted further when Salah came up with an escape plan for Clem, who had long made no secret of his desire to get out. Here, said Salah, was his chance. His idea was to get Clem a forged Bangladeshi travel document. In Clem's car they would drive with an Iraqi colonel to Baghdad where they would drop off the colonel. The two of them would then drive on to the Jordanian border where Clem would go free and Salah would drive Clem's car back to Kuwait.

'Iraqi colonel!' I exclaimed. Salah assured us the man was 'No problem'. In fact, Salah increasingly mentioned Iraqi officers, and that worried me. How did he know them? On the other hand, I knew there were a number of Arabs, including Kuwaitis, who were anxious to save some of their property and were forced to do deals with the Iraqis. Others had had business contacts in Iraq before the invasion, who they thought might now provide them with some kind of protection.

We told Salah that we would consider his plan and decide when he got hold of the Bangladeshi documents. Privately, we thought the idea was ludicrous, but we sensed that an outright rejection might not go down too well. We were dealing with a man whose ego seemed to have grown out of all proportion since the invasion. We wondered why. His confidence did not seem without some basis.

He never brought the forged documents. The last time we saw him we were in no doubt that we were on opposite sides. We nodded politely as he extolled the virtues of Saddam Hussein.

'Kuwait,' he said, 'will never be its own again. It is over. Under Iraqi rule it will prosper. Give it another two months and life will return to normal, and people will forget there ever was a place called Kuwait.'

In the course of the conversation he casually pulled a truncheon from under the white doctor's coat which he continued to wear. 'Don't worry,' he said, brandishing it. 'I am here to help you.' I was worried and I felt no better when he told us he also had a kalashnikov rifle in his car.

Looking back, I realise his behaviour should have signalled danger. But at the time all manner of ideas were being bandied about. Even our Palestinian friends were praising Saddam Hussein for standing up to the Americans. It was an instinctive reaction. They knew they had nothing much to gain from the Iraqi occupation, but Saddam Hussein's sudden championing of the Palestinian cause gave many fresh hopes for their homeland. The more perceptive recognised it for what it was – a way of justifying his invasion and giving it an Arab respectability while rousing local feeling against the American 'infidels'.

The fact that Salah was so obviously in favour of the

invasion which posed such a threat to us did not in itself imply that we might become prisoners. More telling was the motive behind his enthusiasm for it. This, I thought later, wasn't because of any deep affinity he felt for the Iraqi Ba'athist regime, but more the prospect of making some big bucks. He dropped many hints, but, wrapped up in our own predicament, we did not at first read the signs. He had everything, he would tell us. Flats, furniture, food, cars, even cosmetics for me.

'If you decide to move, don't take a lot of luggage with you. I'll provide you with everything you need,' he said.

Now all we wanted was for him just to vanish. As if reading our thoughts, he disappeared. We heard nothing from him for days. And in that time our suspicions of him began to fade. We even felt we may have misjudged him. Ten days went by and then Salah's boss Sameer called. Salah had been fired, he said. He didn't say why, but he advised Clem not to try to call Salah. He couldn't explain over the phone but if Clem were interested he would come over.

'Salah is not to be trusted,' he told Clem.

Clem's first reaction was not to trust either of them. But that same night Salah himself phoned. He sounded as normal as ever. He had been to Baghdad and he asked whether we needed anything. A trip to Baghdad was not unusual for some Arabs: they went there to make international phone calls and do business. By this time we were not sure how to deal with either Salah or Sameer, but I suggested it wouldn't hurt to talk to Sameer. As it happened we never did. There was so much excitement surrounding Nome's departure on September 12 that it was pushed down our list of priorities. On September 13 Salah called again, just to check on us, he said. On Friday September 14 we were arrested.

XIV

A long time ago I discovered that the anticipation of a happy event can be more enjoyable than the experience itself. It was after the invasion that I learned that fear, too, increases with the expectation of danger, but subsides when you are finally face to face with it. For too many weeks I had waited for the soldiers to come and for too many nights I had lain half-awake, expecting the bombs to start falling. There had been so many hours which I felt were somehow borrowed; a debt that, sooner or later, would be called in.

The longest two minutes of anticipation in my life occurred that Friday September 14. Our waiting was about to end. It took that long from the moment George spotted the Red Berets scramble down from their jeeps until they broke down the door of our apartment and poured in. The game was up. The relief did not come straight away, but by the time I had dealt with the practical aspects of being arrested – packing, answering their questions and changing clothes – I had forgotten about fear. I was no longer afraid. The soldiers said they would be taking us to Baghdad. We were to follow in the footsteps of the other hostages. We more or less knew what to expect; we would be taken to Iraqi military installations and kept as human shields against allied air attacks.

As seems always the case before disaster strikes, in the days leading up to Friday our morale had been high. Nome had left safely a couple of days before. Encouraged by the news that my letters were being published in the *Sunday Times*, I was happily tapping away at my computer. Our downstairs neighbours occasionally came up with a plate of homemade pastries and a chat – under the circumstances, everything was fine. Friday is the day of rest in the Arab world and Muslims go to pray at about noon. If ever there was a time to relax, this was it. I washed my hair in the morning and when it was half-dry, instead of putting it in rollers as I usually do, I twisted it strand by strand and secured it with pins.

At about 12.15 Clem and I were in our bedroom. I wore a white lacy dress that looked more like a housecoat. Clem was fiddling with the video recorder when George rushed from the sitting room, rapped on the door and shouted: 'Soldiers, soldiers!' We ran to the hallway. George was coming out of his room. There was no need for questions. I could hear a commotion downstairs and harsh loud voices. George took a step towards the door. I pulled him back, afraid the soldiers would slam it into his face. There was more shouting, then fast footsteps, many of them. There was a knock on the door and the bell rang at the same time. I was standing in the hallway, pressing my back against the wall with my hands pushing hard against it. My body felt as rigid as the wall and my eyes were fixed on the door. Clem was on my right in the doorway of our bedroom. George stood less than a metre away on my left. I looked fleetingly first at one, then the other. Their faces were tense, but I noted that both were composed and in control of themselves. I remember being a little surprised at that. We did not answer the knock or the ring. There was a tremendous bang and the door swung open under somebody's boot. It hit the clothes rail behind it. The soldiers began pouring in, five, ten, about a dozen, their rifles and pistols pointed straight at us.

'Are you Americans? Are you Americans? Do you have weapons? Where are the weapons?' One of them was doing all the shouting in English.

Clem and George said they were Americans. Instinctively, I said I was Yugoslav.

'Is she your wife?' a young captain asked.

'No,' said Clem.

They told us to pack two bags each, and to get ready to go with them. They would take us first to the Regency Palace Hotel, then on to Baghdad. They went into each room, one by one, searching the wardrobes, rummaging through all the drawers. It was the captain who spoke English and who later told us his name was Iyad. But the whole operation was presided over by a tall, fat man dressed like a Kuwaiti. He never spoke to us the whole time they were there.

The captain and the soldiers could barely hide their delight when Clem told them he worked for the Ministry of Defence. Their faces lit up as they babbled to each other in Arabic. They had netted a big fish, they thought. They told him to pack his military manuals and relieved him of them later.

We were about to pack when the phone rang. The captain answered it. I froze.

'Who is speaking?' he asked in English. He turned to us: 'Who is Sandy?' I shrugged my shoulders and said nothing. It was obviously Sandy Macmillan, my British warden. The captain passed the receiver to Clem and the man in the dishdasha pressed the button on the handset which made Sandy's voice audible.

'May I speak to Jadranka Porter?' he said.

'Who?' Clem feigned ignorance to give himself a chance to think. I was silently cursing and willing him to say 'Wrong number.'

When Sandy twice repeated my name I thought

102

'Stupid.' I could foresee the whole network of wardens and people in hiding being cracked by the consequences of all this. Sandy finally got the message and disconnected the line. The captain did not pursue the matter, which was a huge relief.

We began packing while the captain chivvied us to do it faster. 'Hurry up. Hurry up,' he kept shouting, but I noticed he had a smile on his face. While they were waiting, the soldiers went to a floor above. We could hear them breaking into vacant apartments that had been occupied by the German with the binoculars, and two British families who were out of the country when the Iraqis invaded.

I went to my room to change and closed the door behind me. A soldier opened it, saw I was half-dressed, and promptly shut it again. In the bathroom I was bending over my toilet bag, packing some jars of cream, when I suddenly felt a hand on my hip. I jumped a foot. Standing behind me was a soldier. The barrel of his gun was pointed to the floor. He smiled sheepishly and indicated my toothbrush on the shelf above the basin. I smiled back, relieved, and packed the toothbrush. They escorted us downstairs, the captain complaining about the size of my Samsonite suitcase although it was I who was carrying it. In the doorway of the apartment downstairs stood Rawiya, a hard-faced Palestinian woman in her late thirties. She was now close to tears and as I passed her she cried: 'I am sorry. I am sorry.' I smiled at her and told her not to worry. By now we were resigned to our fate. I felt quite calm.

The soldiers were in no way hostile. They even cracked jokes. 'I like the snakes in your hair,' the captain teased. I had not had a chance to brush them out.

I could sense that some of the soldiers were feeling sympathetic towards me as a woman. While we were waiting in the lobby, one of those who had been assigned to guard us offered words of comfort.

'Don't worry,' he said. 'Nothing bad will happen to you.'

By custom Arabs don't enjoy involving women in what they see as men's work, which was how they saw this. But it didn't stop them keeping their guns pointed at my stomach. Now, in the lobby, waiting and watching the soldiers breaking into an empty villa across the road, I began unwinding my hair and brushing it. This made Clem angry and he hissed under his breath: 'Stop doing that, you are provoking them.' We had often discussed the fact that Arabs had a thing about women's hair and I realised this was not the right time to do my coiffure, but I did not expect to enjoy any privacy for a long time and could not go around with my hair in such an outlandish style. To Clem's irritation, the soldiers watched, transfixed.

Everything seemed disorganised. We hung around in the lobby for about fifteen minutes before the captain told us to sit in Clem's car while they went off to search a house at the end of the road. A handful of soldiers were left guarding us. I remembered that I had left my address book in the flat and asked one of the soldiers if I could get it. I went back up to fetch it. Back in the car, I was hot so I got out and paced up and down. A moment or two later I saw a soldier beckoning me from the window of our flat. I again went up. It was a phone call from Zeinab. She was checking on me. I told her I could not talk because there were soldiers around. She got the message. The soldier asked who it was and I gave the name of my Indian friend at the *Arab Times*, Fathima, whom I knew had already left the country. The soldier nodded and I went back to the car.

I was just in time for the return of Captain Iyad and

his men. They were carrying a box full of diving equipment. The captain triumphantly held up a diver's knife and said: 'You see this, it is diving equipment. These people can dive and make contact with your navies in the Gulf.'

He has been watching too many American movies, I thought.

We left in a convoy led by a black Mercedes driven by the fat man, followed by two military trucks and a jeep. Clem drove his car, George sat beside him and I was in the back with a soldier who held a revolver in his hand. We thought we were going straight to the Regency Palace. But as soon as we turned the corner, we all stopped while the soldiers got out to make another search of a house. This time it yielded nothing. There are six ringroads around Kuwait City and we got on to the sixth at the notorious intersection near our home. Clem was told to drive between the two escorting army trucks.

He and George were talking as if they were alone in the car, although the soldier did not seem to understand English.

'I thought we were going to the Regency,' said Clem.

'It doesn't look like it. We are on the Fahaheel expressway,' said George.

'No we are not, we are on the sixth ringroad going west,' said Clem.

'Oh, I know. We are going to the International,' George sounded almost cheerful.

'Well, wherever we are going, we'll get there,' said Clem, indicating the escort.

The soldier by my side was shifting about in his seat at their chatter. I saw him put the revolver into his left hand and with the thumb and the forefinger of his right he pinched his mouth. He looked at me and I nodded.

'Hey, you guys, he wants you to stop talking,' I said.

They didn't say another word.

I was puzzled when we turned towards the Bayan Palace, which was where the government met before the invasion. Its gates were closed but we drove from one to another until two soldiers emerged and opened them. We followed the truck ahead into the palace grounds. We could see the damage from the shelling. It was relatively minor, nothing, I thought, that could not be easily repaired. There were a number of abandoned cars lying around with their bonnets open, and I thought it looked a bit like a used-car lot.

We stopped in the underground parking area. It was empty. It struck me as an odd place to take hostages and I began to feel uneasy. The Iraqis did not seem concerned about us. They got out of their vehicles, walked around and began an animated conversation. Then they got back in and within five minutes we were back on the road.

On the way, I saw the first pictures of Saddam Hussein stuck on the walls. In Surra, about 5 kilometres from the city centre, we stopped again while the soldiers raided a pair of the palatial villas for which this neighbourhood was noted. It was the third time we had seen how they broke into the houses and it was as ugly as the other times. They ran like a wild mob, their rifles held high as they sprinted. Their shouting was like a battle cry. They jumped over the walls, tried to push open the front door. When that failed, one returned to a truck for an iron bar, while others were already getting in through the windows and round the back. One of them got a water bottle and offered it to me. I took a swig. Whatever they had been looking for, they did not seem to have found it and looked disappointed. We seemed to be on a search-and-arrest tour of the whole city. We next went to the Al Kazima sports club on the Damascus Road in Adeliya about 5 kilometres from the city centre. We were told to get out. It was an army command post.

'You are our guests now,' said the captain. We left our luggage and followed the captain inside. He took us first to the office of a colonel. There was a bed in the corner. The colonel was a handsome and well-spoken man in his early forties with grey hair. He told us to sit down and he offered us coffee. He looked at our passports and asked Clem and George where they worked. He told me he had been in Yugoslavia in the 1970s and how much he liked the country. He had even been to my birthplace, a small suburb on the outskirts of Belgrade. He reassured us that we would not be harmed and promised we would be well-treated. He was even apologetic. George, who was hard of hearing, kept moving closer to him and cocking his head to try to understand what the colonel was saying.

Then the captain asked: 'Why didn't you report to the International Hotel when we asked you to?'

'I do what my embassy tells me to do,' Clem said, bravely, I thought.

'But we are now the authority here,' said the captain. Unlike the colonel he was full of himself and hyped up, almost as if he were drunk.

George began to speak of his wife, who, he said, had just left.

'And what about our beloved wives?' interrupted the captain. 'We miss them too.'

George was simply relieved that Nome was now safely back in the States, but the captain pressed on: 'And why didn't you open the door when we came to your place?' he wanted to know.

By this time I had had enough of him. I couldn't keep quiet any longer. 'And how did you arrive – screaming, shouting, pointing guns at us. We are not criminals. We are ordinary, decent people . . .' I said. As a woman I felt I could get away with more than Clem and George, who had sounded rather compliant.

'We are sorry that it happened that way,' the colonel apologised. 'The commander will see you now.'

Down the corridor we were shown into the commander's office. He sat behind a big desk, a short slim man with straight black oiled hair. He also looked about forty. He did not speak English, and a man in civilian clothes, sitting close by, translated. We later learned he was a member of Mukhabarat, the Iraqi secret police.

They concentrated on Clem and asked him what he did. He told them he was an instructor and they asked him details of his training programme. Clem was talking rubbish all the time; he said the same thing in about ten different ways. They asked him about George's job while George was sitting next to him. They wanted to know how we got our food and who provided it. It was then that Clem began telling them about the network of helpers organised by the US Embassy. I thought: 'Damn fool. He can get them all arrested.'

I quickly interrupted. 'I did the shopping,' I said.

'All the time?' asked the translator.

'Yes, several times and each time I bought a lot,' I told him.

Now it was the commander's turn to interrupt in Arabic. 'Mara, mara?' ('What about the woman?')

But instead of asking me, the translator asked Clem about me.

I was now regretting that we had not arranged our story in advance, but I decided to speak for myself. Before Clem could say any more, I began talking. I told them I was a teacher of English, and I was on a visit from Yugoslavia. My Yugoslav friends in Kuwait had been unable to take me with them when they left and had put me up with Clem and George.

'I don't believe you,' said the secret policeman.

I do a very good line in shrugs and I gave him one.

Thankfully, the commander was engrossed in his other work. He seemed only to be half-listening and he was also making and receiving phone calls. Visitors kept popping in and out and, in between, he was signing papers. It was reminiscent of one of my many frustrating newspaper interviews with Kuwaiti government officials, who always managed to do three jobs at once and give scant attention to me. This time, though, I had no objection. My only fear was that one of the orderlies might walk into the office with my British passport and I would be exposed. The passport was in my bag in the car.

The interview finally came to an end after about twenty minutes. Before leaving, the commander told us that we had been detained for our own protection against 'dangerous elements' in Kuwait who would want to kill us. He did not make clear who they might be. The American Embassy, he said, would not care if we got killed and he implied that the United States was looking for just such a pretext to attack Iraq. The obnoxious little captain also had a word of advice for me. In the presence of Clem and George he said: 'Keep away from Americans. They destroyed socialism throughout eastern Europe. They don't treat people well, not even their own,' he said, motioning at Clem. I wasn't going to argue.

Soon we were on the road again, this time in an army jeep and finally heading for the Regency Palace. Captain Iyad was driving, his pistol on the seat between his legs. He was extremely cheerful and persuaded his companion, Ra'ad, who was carrying a rifle, to sing some bedouin songs. It was bizarre. Ra'ad howled at the top of his voice while Iyad urged him to sing another song. In the process, he lost his way and the three of us looked at each other incredulously. It was as if we were on a joyride. What on earth was going on?

George tried to interrupt. 'Lieutenant – ' he began, only to be cut off in midstream.

'I am not a lieutenant. I am a captain.'

George immediately apologised and volunteered that he was from Nevada.

'Oh, Nevada. You have the desert there, but, unlike us, you cannot survive in the desert,' said the captain smugly. He made me feel sick.

At the Regency Palace the secret police were in charge. There was not a uniform in sight but some of the Mukhabarat wore holsters on their trouserbelts. One of them came up to us as we entered and asked for our passports. I showed him mine and he said I was free to go. I was astonished. After all I had gone through, to arrive at my destination and be told to go was almost an anticlimax. In my mind I was all prepared to go to Baghdad, set for a new experience. Now it was not to be. At the same time, I felt an obvious sense of relief. All this went through my mind while the man looked at George's and Clem's passports, then told them to check in.

What we feared most was now happening, not the prospect of going to Baghdad, but being separated. It was awful, but all over so quickly. Clem and George were busy at the reception desk and although I know he must have felt emotion, Clem didn't say anything. It was so confusing when the moment came to say goodbye. I kissed George on the cheek but I didn't even kiss Clem, nor he me. We both seemed to feel inhibited by the presence of others around us and the fact that this was the Arab world, which places severe constraints on any open display of affection. I was also aware that we had told the Iraqis we were not husband and wife, and that I was just a guest in their flat. Under other circumstances we would have flung our arms around each other. Instead, and absurdly, we just shook hands and said goodbye in the lobby. I saw them disappear towards the lifts. I felt drained and very tired. I sat down and asked one of the hotel staff to find me a cigarette. I felt as limp as a puppet, wondering who was going to pull my strings next.

It turned out to be Captain Iyad. One of the hotel staff asked him if he would give me a lift home, but instead he told me to go to the dining room and have lunch. He told me to go back to the flat at about 7 p.m. I wondered why. It was now only 3.30. But I was too tired to argue. It seemed as though he had given me some orders, so I got up and walked to the dining room. I looked around, wondering where to sit. All the tables were empty. Then a man walked up to me. His face was vaguely familiar and he said he was the general manager. I told him I wanted to go home, and he took me back to the lobby and spoke to one of the Mukhabarat people, who said I could leave immediately. But the Iraqis had taken Clem's car and I had no transport. The manager told one of his staff, a Lebanese man called Assef, to drive me home. It took only about three or four minutes, and, when we arrived, there was a jeep parked in front of the gate. It was Captain Iyad's.

XV

As I walked through the gate into the house, my down-stairs neighbours came to meet me. Three soldiers were in my flat, they said. Mohammed and I were climbing the stairs when a soldier came out of my flat with a gun and stopped us. He shouted something and Captain Iyad appeared. He told me that they had to search the flat, and to wait downstairs. He would call me when they were finished. While I waited, my neighbours invited Assef and me in for coffee. There were about ten of them in the flat and they wanted to hear my story. I told them briefly what had happened. They had been shaken by the raid at noon and now were noticeably subdued. I think they were concerned that, during the questioning, we might have implicated them in some way. I reassured them. They were also convinced that we had been betrayed because when the soldiers had arrived, they had told them they were looking for four Americans, one of them black.

My neighbours wondered who the traitor was. At the time I had not even considered it. They suspected one of the Egyptian watchmen in the neighbourhood. Then Omar's stepmother, Maha, said something that puzzled me.

'We had expected the soldiers on Thursday.'

Why should they expect them at all? I wondered, but I was too numb and tired to ask.

'It had to happen sooner or later,' said her husband.

It didn't *have* to, I wanted to say, but thought better of

it. I was glad to have company but this family, I felt, was courteous, but nothing more.

I waited for Captain Iyad. An hour passed and there was no sign of him. Omar's father went out. 'The jeep is gone,' he said. We rushed upstairs and into the flat. I walked from room to room, everything had been turned upside-down. Three video recorders were missing – they had left the bulky Betamax – the cameras were gone, so had a carton of cigarettes and my alarm clock. The papers, books, Clem's computer, and dozens of his discs were untouched. It had not been a search but a robbery, which was why they had left so quietly. My neighbours shook their heads in disbelief and quietly left me alone.

I went into the bedroom and sat on the bed. Then the agony began. It was as if I had been beaten and thumped all over. My chest felt tight. I did not know what to do. I remembered Clem and needed to know that he and George had not been harmed. I thought of them being interrogated and tortured and felt sick. I missed them so much. All my worries about my relationship with Clem seemed to melt away. I just could not bear to think of the ordeal they might be going through.

When the phone rang it was someone called Mike from the American Embassy. I explained what had happened and he was sympathetic. He would try to get in touch with George and Clem at the Regency. I refrained from calling anyone, in case our phone had been tapped. Much later, Sandy, my warden, called. Though I didn't know him well, I poured my heart out to him. He got in touch with a British girl, Lorraine, and asked her to call me because he thought it would help to have a woman-to-woman talk. It was thoughtful, and she was nice, but she was a stranger and I craved to talk to Clem.

I decided to call him but before I could pick up the

phone, it rang. It was him. He sounded fine. They were being well treated and had just had dinner. He was more worried about me and was afraid that soldiers might come back at night to steal and even rape. They knew I was alone. I had already thought of the possibility and arranged with my downstairs neighbours that I would immediately rush down to them if the soldiers came to the front door. Assef, my driver from the hotel, had also warned me of the possibility of rape. He advised me to leave for Baghdad as soon as possible. I didn't know at the time what his motives might be.

Rape was one of the topics most discussed after the invasion. Within days, stories were circulating about a dozen cases. Apart from the British stewardess and the German woman, there had also been stories involving Arab and Filipino women. There were reports that several Filipino women in the Mubarak Hospital hostel, and others in the Al Muthana complex in the city, had been assaulted. Later, an Englishman, Tom Lemming, told me how he had prevented the rape of a Sri Lankan woman. She and her husband were staying with Tom after fleeing their flat. One day Tom returned from the shops to find her husband outside the closed bedroom door. Tom rushed in and found the woman on the bed and an Iraqi soldier bent over her. Tom shouted at the soldier in Arabic and he left.

Ski told me about a Pakistani family who were trying to escape through the desert to Saudi Arabia. They were stopped near the border by an Iraqi patrol who forced the parents across the border into Saudi Arabia, but detained their two teenage daughters. They raped the girls for two days before sending them to the city.

By December a gynaecologist working at one of the city hospitals had reports of 160 cases of rape from various sources, most of them Arabs. Like many other women, I had never believed it could happen to me. Now I wasn't so sure.

I began to anticipate the prospect. How would I protect myself, now that I was alone? If my neighbours were being held at gunpoint they would not be in a position to help me. If it did happen, how would I cope with the pain? When I decided to stay on in Kuwait I made up my mind that the moment I felt I was becoming psychologically damaged, and that there would be scars, I would pack my bags and leave. Now I wondered whether, after the night ahead, it would be too late for that. I sat for hours in the darkness, watching the street. I vowed not to fall asleep. I rehearsed in my mind what might happen if the soldiers did come. I thought that, if I was prepared, I would be less damaged by the experience.

I imagined them stomping into the apartment as they had that morning, screaming and shouting, throwing me on the bed, ripping off my clothes. I decided it would be pointless to resist. But though they could violate my body, they would not control my mind. That was a pleasure I could deny them. I would turn my head away and shut my mind to their brutality. I would think of anything, of my family. No, not my family, it had to be something impersonal. I would think of my travels, yes, my trekking in the Himalayas, of green fields and mountain streams, of that floating island in the lake in Seraj, 3000 metres above sea level. I was actually far from sure that I would be able to cut myself off from the reality with such images. I was afraid I would just go limp with fear and become an easy toy in their hands. I did not know how to pray. 'Please, don't come,' I silently implored.

It was about three in the morning when, exhausted and almost beyond caring, my vigil ended and I fell asleep. When I woke up four hours later the world seemed like a dark pit with me at the bottom of it. I reached for the phone, dialled the Regency Palace, and asked for Room 338. Clem answered. He had not slept a wink and George had not gone to bed until five. They had spent the night talking to other hostages and listening to the news.

I got up and, wherever I looked, there was a reminder of Clem. His tennis shoes were on the floor, his toiletries were still in the bathroom and I couldn't bear to go into the kitchen because this was where I best remembered him. I had never been in this flat alone for any great length of time and now I wanted him back with all my heart and all his faults. I began tidying up, hoovering furiously, and giving the pots and pans a scrub such as they had never had before. I remembered the Vietnam pilot's advice to hostages: take one day at a time. One day! It should be more like one minute. I reached for the phone again, to call Clem. 'Sorry ma'am, we have orders not to put anyone through to 338,' said the receptionist.

This was the end. What's going on in his room? What are they doing to him? An hour later, Clem called. He could phone out, but could not receive calls.

He had a question: 'Will you marry me?'

I swallowed. I was in no state to make such decisions. All I wanted was for him to be safe. By the time I had explained, I was in tears. I cried so much I was unable to speak. I lost all will to fight back the tears. Clem said that Assef would come round in the afternoon and would I please send him some of his books, his underwear and the adaptor for his radio. I set about packing a bag for him, and immediately felt better. I tried to think of all the things he might need and gathered them all together: radio batteries, a writing pad, vitamins and body lotion. I also packed two bottles of his favourite Bourbon. I searched the house for something that could be a present from me, a lucky charm. I found an onyx rabbit and I wrote a note saying I hoped he would soon be free.

Salah called in the early afternoon. I told him what had happened. He did not sound surprised and he promised to go to see Clem at the hotel.

Bob Morris, an American friend, who was hiding in the Al Muthana complex, also called. He spoke in a whisper, like many of my callers, but this time with good reason. Bob suggested that Clem might want to escape from the hotel and he had hatched a plan. I was to tell Clem to go to the hotel gym and to jog on the track for two successive afternoons. On the third, he should run through the gym door on to the Gulf road where somebody would be waiting in a car to pick him up.

'I just want him to have an option,' Bob said.

I promised to try to pass the message on to Clem, but it sounded like a hare-brained scheme to me. In any case, Assef had told me the Iraqis were listening in on phone calls at the Regency. I could not bring myself to tell Clem. I was afraid if the Iraqis got wind of it we would all suffer. More than that, Clem could be shot attempting to escape. When Assef came in the afternoon I felt listless. Clem had sent me a letter and KD 100 ($360). I was still debating whether to write him a note mentioning the escape plan, but I was not sure if I could trust Assef. I watched him shamelessly snooping around the flat and I trusted him less and less. He got out the old Betamax and connected it to the television. I was in no mood for videos. He connected the hi-fi as well and played some music. I think he was checking to see if the equipment worked.

'I know someone who would take you to Baghdad, and I can sell your stuff,' he said.

Here was I, distraught with grief, and he was busy calculating the resale value of our possessions. I began to get angry, but I knew I could not afford to antagonise him. He could help us or hurt us. It depended on how I

117

played it. It would be best to keep him hopeful while Clem was still in the hotel. I told him I did not feel well enough to travel, but he would be the first to know when I decided to leave for Baghdad.

I read Clem's letter. He loved me, he said, but we could never be happy together. 'For your own happiness, I have to let you go. Maybe this event has done it for us,' he wrote. This could all be true but I couldn't cope with it now. When was this emotional roller-coaster going to stop? There had to be a better time to deal with it.

That night I sat by the window again, although I had begun to sense the soldiers would not come back.

Over the next three days my mood swung wildly and frequently. Despair was followed by relief, then despair again. Then Clem called. He had discovered who had betrayed us. Salah. He never went to visit Clem and although Clem tried to phone him many times, he could never find him. Clem had spoken with several British hostages whom we had met at a Christmas party for which Salah had done the catering. They were convinced that it was Salah who had brought the soldiers to their houses. One of them claimed he actually saw Salah in front of his house when the soldiers came to arrest him. Like us, they had all been in touch with him in the weeks leading up to their arrest. A Frenchman who had worked for Salah had also been betrayed. Both Clem and I were not too surprised and, in any case, it was too late to think about what might have been. But I gave Salah's name to Sandy my warden and it was passed around to others in hiding. I was told his name was also being given to Kuwaiti resistance fighters. I never saw or spoke to Salah again. I don't even know whether he is still alive.

As for Clem, he was taken to Baghdad at 11 a.m. on Tuesday September 19, four days after his arrest. That morning he called me every half hour until he left in a bus. Sameer had apparently tried to persuade the Iraqis to keep Clem, and the Frenchman he knew, detained at the Regency and an hour before he left, Clem still held out hope he would not be taken away.

I called Sameer. 'Would it help if we got married?' I asked.

He said it would not. 'I'm sorry. I tried, but there is nothing I can do,' he said.

When the time came to part on the phone, I was in tears. 'Take good care of yourself, stay strong and don't lose the rabbit,' I managed between sobs.

When he had gone I sank into deep depression. I was disorientated and terribly lonely. Once again I remembered the American pilot's survival rule: 'No matter how much you hurt, you should try to help others.' I picked up the phone and called Eoin MacDougald. As a Canadian, he was able to move around freely, although he was not allowed to leave the country. He was our Mr Fix-it. He distributed food among those in hiding. He picked up mail and he knew where to go to photocopy documents or to find computer paper for those who used it.

'Eoin, if you need any help, I am ready,' I said.

Within days a whole new life began.

XVI

When it came, our arrest – the boot in the door, the guns and the shouts, the interrogation, the way that Clem and George had been torn away from me – was shattering; though I knew that other people had been taken away in similar circumstances and, in the case of Kuwaitis, often more brutally. They were the victims of the harshest measures. Iraqi soldiers, fired by fresh orders to neutralise any signs of unrest, were constantly kicking in doors, searching houses and taking away their occupants for the slightest breach of the new rules. Anyone caught with a picture in their home of an Al Sabah was a traitor. The punishment was often summary and applied at the discretion of the officer in charge. Teenagers caught daubing anti-Saddam slogans were among the main sufferers. Some were caught in the act and shot on the spot. Others were bundled off to detention where they were acccused of resistance activities. Some were tortured to reveal the names of members of the resistance, who the Iraqis claimed had incited them. A favourite method of terror was for soldiers to break into a house and round up the servants. They would point pistols to their heads and demand to know which members of the family were in the resistance, or were Kuwaiti army officers who had gone into hiding or switched into civilian clothes.

The children were particularly vulnerable. They would be asked such questions as: 'What does your daddy do? Did he used to wear a uniform? Where is he now?' Frightened and unsure of what was happening, the children would unwittingly give information which could end up with the arrest, detention and often torture of those suspected of resisting the occupation forces. As time went on, parents began coaching their children to avoid such questioning. Saddam Hussein's name became sacred, along with his picture, which by now was mushrooming on walls and prominent sites around the city. He had assumed godlike proportions, and anything said against him was an invitation to immediate arrest and detention. So fearful were the Kuwaitis of reprisals if they were overheard saying anything critical about him, that they were constantly looking over their shoulder and speaking in hushed tones, even in their own homes. They impressed on their children the need not to repeat anything they might overhear in the home or on the street. People even became wary of speaking against Saddam to friends and neighbours with whom they had formerly been on intimate terms. Trust was not generously bestowed because the consequences could be so dire if misplaced.

The aim of the Iraqis was clear. When popular support for their presence was not forthcoming, they were quick to introduce terror tactics to force the population to submit to the new rule. This forcible attempt to assimilate Kuwaitis into the Iraqi population by making them pay homage to the Saddam regime had a double purpose. On the one hand there was the need to cut loyalty to the Kuwaiti ruling family whom they were told had deserted them. On the other, there was the need to wipe out all sense of nationality and to brainwash them into taking on new identities as Iraqis. Kuwait had been declared Iraq's 19th Province and had no past history. To achieve this, the Iraqis dealt with any sign of dissent with an iron fist and a bullet in the head. Lima's sister at Mubarak Hospital told of seeing six bodies of resistance fighters being brought to the hospital in the first week of September. They had all been shot in the head. Twelve others were shot dead after their cars were stopped at roadblocks, and weapons allegedly found. But the Iraqis did not always need a pretext to mete out punishment.

I wrote on October 1: 'Whatever misfortune has befallen the foreigners, it is incomparable to the atrocities committed against the Kuwaitis. It is they who have been mounting attacks on the Iraqis and bearing the brunt of Iraqi reprisals. Ten young Kuwaitis, three of them on the Adan Hospital staff, were arrested and killed. Their bodies were dumped in front of their homes. Other hospital reports say that Kuwaitis have been brought in with parts of their fingers missing. Another was admitted with one eyeball hanging out. The manager of the Ardiya Co-operative supermarket was shot dead in the shop itself, allegedly for manipulating the prices. In Rowda, a Kuwaiti neighbourhood, the Iraqis who came under attack from the resistance blew up three houses, one used by snipers and one on each side.'

The Kuwaitis began quietly collecting information about family and individual loyalties, and compiling blacklists. It was becoming increasingly clear that once the nightmare was over and the Kuwaitis were again back in charge there would be a horrible settling of accounts, and heads would literally roll.

Westerners had always been culturally separated from the Kuwaitis and this had turned into a physical separation when we went into hiding, so it took a long time for what the Kuwaitis were suffering to filter through. When it did, we were brought instinctively closer together. With the West by now actively seeking the restoration of Kuwait's independence, the two communities automatically found themselves in the same camp. But the identity of purpose was only one factor. More important was that both communities were being persecuted and this forged a fresh bond between them. In the past, individual friendships notwithstanding, the relationship was governed by business and financial interests. The Kuwaitis may not have liked the Westerners much but they respected their expertise. The Westerners had little respect for the Kuwaitis, who were seen to be the idle beneficiaries of the Westerners' efforts. All that had now changed. The courage that ordinary Kuwaitis had displayed since the invasion was an eye opener. Holed up and frightened, we needed help, and the Kuwaitis, as well as Indians, Palestinians and others, delivered this help. The conflict brought out the worst in some people, but it brought out the best in others, and a wonderful sense of community that cut across racial, national and cultural differences.

I was one of the few women of any nationality living alone. I had been on the run, detained, I had lost my closest friends and had been trying to protect myself from threats which seemed at the time to be lurking around every corner. I was still feeling low over the loss of Clem. I had not heard from him in the two weeks since he was taken away. I was suffering from attacks of profound anxiety. They were like seizures that suddenly gripped me and I had to make a conscious effort not to think about what had happened and not to concentrate on his predicament, whatever that might be. I was in a bad way, but the people I knew – some of whom I had yet to meet face-to-face – were supremely supportive: offering words of comfort, food, shelter and sending friends round to keep me company.

Support for me came in from all sides. Mike Penneman was among those to show understanding. He was an executive director of Merrill Lynch and was on a visit to Kuwait when the Iraqis invaded. Since then he had taken refuge in the American Embassy. When I complained that my neighbours were courteous but since the arrest had become distant, he said: 'They are only being prudent.' I was finding it hard to be objective about the way people behaved. He promised to send someone around to talk to me but, by then, my other friends were rallying round. Bob Morris, a dentist who was also in hiding, phoned regularly. He would say such things as: 'We are thinking of you, we are with you.' Bill Van Rye and many others offered me a place I could move to where I wouldn't be alone. But moving was hazardous. With the Iraqis on the streets, the risk of being picked up again was too great. I also needed time to heal, and for that I needed to retreat into my own nest. Bill, at first, felt he should have been able to prevent our arrest. He had organised a network of contacts soon after the invasion. They monitored Iraqi troop movements and house searches and were often able to give an hour's warning to someone in hiding before a search took place. When he was not informed in advance of our arrest, he began to suspect a mole in his network. There was, however, one situation when the system could not function. If we were betrayed by someone outside the network, it would not know of it. I told him I thought we had been turned in, and to some extent he was relieved. At this time there were still hundreds of Westerners in hiding and, to them, his early-warning system could mean the difference between staying a fugitive and being taken as a human shield.

Although Ski never called after our arrest, his Kuwaiti friend Abdul Latif Shamali did. I assumed Ski kept silent for his own security, fearing my phone may have been bugged. For a while I even thought the Iraqis might have released me so that I would lead them to other Westerners in hiding. My first visitors after the arrest, apart from my neighbours, were Zeinab and her Kuwaiti husband Kahtan. He was twenty years older than Zeinab and although she had a heart of gold I felt she was basically unhappy, trying unsuccessfully to escape the straitjacket that Kuwaiti custom imposed on women. Her husband was of Iraqi origin and he had relatives in Basra and Baghdad. That day Zeinab told me: 'He is all the way for Kuwait. He would give his last blood for Kuwait.' Kahtan was planning a trip to Basra and promised to bring me back some vegetables and beer. Although I did not see much of them because they lived well north of the city, they would remain supportive and trusted friends right up to their tragic death, a day before the liberation.

The two people who did most to prop me up and who became indispensable friends were the Scot and the Canadian, Sandy Macmillan and Eoin MacDougald. Both had had similar experiences to my own. Eoin, an architect in his early forties, had been arrested and taken to the Regency Palace after trying to escape to the border in the early days of the invasion. He had been released because he was Canadian, but his British friends, who had tried to escape with him, were kept in detention and this gnawed away at his conscience.

Sandy, a red-haired engineer, was dragged forcibly by Iraqi soldiers from a supermarket after a raid in search of resistance fighters. He left the building with his hands above his head, a gun stuck into his ribs. 'I nearly wet my pants,' he laughed at the recollection. His stories helped to keep my spirits up. More than twenty years before, he told me, while working on an archaeological site at Winchester Cathedral, his team excavated a mass grave containing scores of skeletons at least 500 years old. The discovery required the presence of an official from the Vatican to confirm it. At the site of the skeletons, the official said to the archaeologists, in all seriousness:

'Please be sure to separate the Catholics from the Prot-
estants.'

Despite these diversions, the Iraqi presence was always
with us, though not all the stories of Western encounters
with soldiers were distressing. Eoin wrenched his video
recorder away from an Iraqi soldier during what the Canadian called a 'commercial visit' to his home. On the
same visit Eoin was arguing in the garden with an officer,
trying to stop them stealing his car when a soldier began
taking away his hi-fi and video system. 'Hey, wait a
minute, that's mine,' shouted Eoin. The soldier obedi-
ently took it back inside and, when he came out again,
the officer went up to him and slapped him round the
face. Then he smiled at Eoin as if to say: 'There, I have
punished him.'

Such episodes portrayed the Iraqis as less menacing
than they were. Was it possible that in our fear and isolation we had invested them with a power and a brutality
they did not possess? The thought hardly survived its
emergence. There was enough evidence to the contrary
from the hundreds of stories I had heard and, indeed,
from my own experience. Still, I began to feel less threatened – it had something to do with my new perception of
fear. I recalled one of those slogans at salesmen's seminars
which said that a truly successful person was one who
could turn an adverse situation into one of advantage. I
had one experience under my belt which I knew should
make me stronger, not weaker. Now I was going to prove
that this was the case.

The first thing I needed was to get mobile. Eoin set
about getting my car registration book forged using my
maiden name and my Yugoslav nationality. The Iraqis
had released me as a Yugoslav and so it was obvious I
should continue to stay one. This way I could move
around freely whereas, as a Briton, I could be detained,

interrogated, and even shot as a spy for my reports to the *Sunday Times*. At best, I would have been deported, which was now the last thing I wanted.

Kuwait was in a state of lawlessness and the Iraqis did not seem accountable for any crimes they committed. My Yugoslav passport seemed my most reliable safety net so long as I maintained a low profile. I began slowly coming into my own again. I had my writing and as soon as I could drive again, I could start repaying the visits of those who had come to see me by going to see others who had not been so fortunate.

XVII

It took ten days for Eoin to fix my registration book and that same day I went out for the first time since my arrest almost three weeks before. My first visit was to see Diana Elias, a Lebanese journalist, and her family. She was afraid to do any writing after an Arab girlfriend was detained when the Iraqis discovered her diary. Living above Diana was Richard Hattersley, the Jabriya warden, who had urged us not to go to the International Hotel as ordered by the Iraqis. He lived with two other Britons, Dean and Archie, and an Irishman, Raymond, who was nicknamed Rachel because of his skill in the kitchen. They were in good spirits, though I found it difficult to cope with their accents. Richard from Newcastle clipped his words so sharply, he sounded as though he was speaking shorthand. Archie had a stammer as well as a strong Scottish accent, while Rachel had a thick Irish brogue. But they were a wonderful group and had prepared a banquet of spaghetti bolognese. We sat chatting for hours, mainly about our own predicament, which led us to one of the topics uppermost in the minds of many Britons. Why had the British Embassy failed to warn us of the invasion, and why did it seem so unprepared to deal with it when it came?

Richard had some surprising information. The warden network which kept expatriates in touch with each other and their embassy had apparently existed throughout the Iraq–Iran war in case it should spill over into Kuwait. But four days before the invasion all the wardens were called to the embassy where the ambassador, Michael Weston, told them that the Iraqis might well cross the border but would stop for about ten days at the Mutla Ridge about half an hour's drive from the city. There they would 'rattle their sabres' and demand the Kuwaitis 'pay up'. Presumably this meant acceding to the Iraqi demands made during the course of the dispute. Their troops would then withdraw. Someone asked the ambassador whether he should bring his holiday forward from August 5 to August 1 but the ambassador had said no. The embassy told Britons that if they were planning to move their dependents out of Kuwait they should do so as quietly as possible, although the embassy did not think it was necessary.

Only after the invasion were the wardens provided with the list of British residents in the country. Richard showed me his list. It was dated October 1987 and when he tried to locate them, more than half had left the country in the years between. Richard updated his list by stationing himself in front of the local co-op, going up to any likely Westerner and asking: 'Are you British?' Sandy Macmillan dealt with the same problem in a different way. He put the word about that anyone wanting to be evacuated should contact him. He was flooded with calls and as a result both wardens were able to compile full up-to-date lists of Britons in their area.

We were all appalled at the failure of Western intelligence to anticipate the invasion, especially as Saddam had signalled it enough times. But I was more shocked to learn that the British Embassy had expected an Iraqi incursion to the Mutla Ridge but did nothing to warn the British community. Not everyone agreed with me. Dean argued that the fact that I was in Kuwait had nothing to do with the British government and that, since we were here through personal choice, we were responsible for ourselves. I saw the role of the embassy not merely as representing the interests of its government but also giving protection to its people. I had had a blazing row with Sandy about it. He blamed the plight of Britons on their failure to register. How was the embassy supposed to reach those, including myself, who hadn't made their presence in Kuwait known? 'What could they do?' he asked. I suggested that when they learnt of the Iraqi incursion, they could have put a small ad in the *Arab Times*, urging people to register. The embassy had much better access to information than we had, and was in a far better position to assess the danger. I held the embassy more responsible for what it failed to do before the invasion, than its loss of control, contact and the confusion immediately afterwards. I had tried several times to phone the embassy in the early days but it was not till the fourth day that I made contact, after a BBC broadcast. I was told to keep on listening to the BBC. About three days later I called again and they gave me the name of my warden. From then on the warden network worked very well, keeping us in touch with other Britons, ensuring we had enough food and, when the evacuations were finally arranged, that we knew about them. They also gave us a lot of moral support over the phone, although they themselves were in hiding and couldn't make visits.

We were still aggrieved, however, that the embassy, or the wardens, had not passed on the knowledge that the invasion could be imminent. The wardens said this was because they had no up-to-date list of residents, but I felt more effort should have been made. They may have been afraid of causing panic but that would have been preferable to being trapped inside Kuwait. The panic would have lasted a day or so, while people got out, not four months, while they remained trapped. In some ways what was even more disturbing was what the embassy did with its knowledge once it knew an Iraqi incursion was expected. It must have passed this on to the British Foreign Office, so why did the latter fail to act? In turn, the British Foreign Office would surely have informed the Americans, if they did not already know from contacts at embassy level in Kuwait. Apparently both embassies had similar meetings about the Iraqi threat, though there were rumours later that the British only called theirs because the Americans had held a meeting. Did the Americans hear of the planned incursion first and pass it on to the British? Or did they each hear separately through their own sources? The US Embassy and the State Department were themselves sending out conflicting signals. The embassy advised us, via Clem's company, to stay indoors on that first morning. But the State Department message, broadcast on the Voice of America two days later, advised people to leave. Britain meanwhile was telling people to stay indoors. Soon after, so were the Americans.

The confusion was rife. When, on the second or third day, Bob Morris became one of the first Americans to be detained, he managed to flee from the Sheraton Hotel, where he was being held, and phoned his embassy. He told the people there that Americans were being rounded up, but they did not believe him. Bill Van Rye, another American, confirmed Bob's story and said: 'The embassy had no idea of what was going on.' The embassy finally called a meeting and it was obvious that Americans *were* being detained. Bill attended the meeting at which the embassy staff were making reassuring noises and telling everyone there was no cause for concern. When the meeting ended, Bill walked with a friend across from the embassy to the International Hotel where they said goodbye to each other. As Bill's friend walked into the lobby, he was promptly arrested and became one of the first human shields. Such incidents shook our confidence in our embassies.

The French, however, seemed to be more in tune with what was going on. Of seven diplomats in Kuwait at the time of the invasion under the Chargé d'Affaires, four were retained in the embassy building while the other three were sent to live with the French community, so that links could be maintained. While the French were deploying their staff in this way, at least five of the American Embassy staff were holed up in the Japanese Embassy.

Unlike the British, the Americans never managed to get their warden system off the ground, partly because there seemed to be little co-ordination between the British and American embassies. More than three months after the invasion, Sandy Macmillan received a fax message from Gale Rogers, the US consul. She had only just learned that a number of British wardens were still functioning and expressed herself delighted at the news. I couldn't believe that she was so out of touch. It seemed to prove how detached the US Embassy was from the situation outside its own compound. Soon after, the American counsellor, Barbara Bodin, told Eoin the embassy was only then thinking of setting up its own warden system. It never happened, because events overtook them.

All this time the British warden service was working wonders. Sandy, who was mine until he left with the other hostages in December, was always available on the phone to perk up our spirits. He also put his own personal safety at risk, regularly phoning Britons detained at the Regency Palace, even though the hotel lines were tapped. He also received many visitors which could have given away his presence and led to his arrest. He was a staunch defender of the embassy and I must admit it went a long way towards redeeming itself when it returned to active service immediately after the liberation. About thirty Britons who survived from day one were given easy access to the ambassador, who treated them warmly. He even arranged for them to meet the Prime Minister, John Major, when he landed by helicopter within days of the Iraqi withdrawal. We were supplied with all manner of things which we thought the Kuwaitis would bring in first, including portable generators, gas cylinders, lamps and food and water. It was an impressively efficient display and they were ahead of other embassies by a mile. I was for once touched by and proud of Britain and I rushed over to tell my American neighbour Karl and to ask him how he had fared at the American Embassy. He gave me a wry smile and said: 'They told me to come back in a week, when they've got themselves organised.'

XVIII

I was by now not so floored by my separation from Clem
and was anxious to become an active part of the
community-in-hiding. But when I joined the unofficial
network of helpers it was as much in response to calls
from people in need as it was to any initiative taken by
me. I had relied heavily on help from outside and now I
wanted to do my share. People would call and ask me to
talk to them. They were plainly depressed by their isolation and needed to speak to someone, if only to vent
their frustration and desperation. Others were living in
pairs or groups and had begun quarrelling, and they
needed someone to complain to and take their side.
Their problems were the same as Clem's and mine had
been. They rowed over one being less security-conscious
than another, one was using the phone too much and
they thought the Iraqis would detect them. They were
just getting on each other's nerves. Some were fussy
about the way they lived, others were content to live in
a more careless fashion. They were like the Odd Couple,
thrown together by force of circumstance rather than
choice and compatibility. One thing they did have in common was a hunger for information about what was happening outside. With my new-found mobility I was in
touch with people of all nationalities, including Kuwaitis,
and as a result my knowledge about what was going on
increased. I passed this on in phone calls and visits to
those in hiding. Not that I was not still at risk. I kept a
close watch on roadblocks in Salwa and frequently

exchanged information on troop movements with Eoin, who lived close by.

At first, the Iraqis set up checkpoints on the main highways. But these caused traffic jams so they decided to make only random checks to keep the traffic flowing. It was when they moved the checkpoints to side roads that we found ourselves in trouble. We were using the same side roads to avoid their checkpoints. Now we had to find new routes. By October, checkpoints were set up on all entry roads into Salwa, and the entire neighbourhood was under tight surveillance. For a time I kept mainly within the area. Most of my friends lived in Salwa, where more than a hundred Westerners were hiding. I knew where almost all the checkpoints were and avoided them by driving through alleys and across patches of wasteground. Then they moved the roadblocks again. My documents were only enough to get me through roadblocks so long as the soldiers were not too careful about checking them. I was also conspicuous as a Western woman. The surprised stares I got from other motorists and soldiers when I first went out made me self-conscious. If someone did examine my papers closely I was almost certainly to be taken for questioning. As a woman without a job and husband, I would have had a hard time explaining why I was still in the country. As Salwa was under tight surveillance, I could not come back into the area without being seen and checked. I was hoping that the more I moved about, the more familiar I would become to them and the less suspicious I would look, but it could easily work the other way.

It wasn't only checkpoints I had to worry about. If I was on a night trip, there was always the risk of running into a patrol. I was driving home one night along the Gulf coast road when I ran slap into one. I stopped and said to the lieutenant in charge: 'I know, I know I broke the

135

curfew.' He said he didn't mind and instead asked me: 'Do you have any cigarettes? We are three smokers.' I gave him what I had and drove off.

I was becoming increasingly expert in supplying food and mail to my charges. I had begun baking bread for myself and started a delivery service. I also helped to collect mail from those in hiding and delivered it when it came from overseas via embassies in Baghdad and Jordan. The mail quite often ended up at the Kiwi house in Salwa which had been occupied by New Zealanders until they left the country. It was a hiding place for a number of British fugitives over the months, but it also became an unofficial meeting place for those willing to take risks to go out. This was partly because it was occupied by Lise-lotte Hertz, an attractive Danish girl who had moved in when the Kiwis left. Having worked for more than ten years in Kuwait, she knew the country and people well. She was lively and got along well with everyone, and it was not unnatural that she should become the focal point, especially as she herself had been busy making contact with many of those in hiding.

The Kiwi house soon became a kind of headquarters for distribution of mail, food and money, which was now being donated by Kuwaitis. They had arranged their own network for their people in need and when they became aware of the plight of Westerners in hiding, they arranged to make donations to them, too. I began to drop in almost daily, after collecting mail from my parishioners. From there it was passed on to messengers carrying mail to Baghdad, from where it would be handed in to embassies who would then send it on in their diplomatic bags. Some of it would go to Jordan where it was posted.

Initially Sandy organised the mailing service to and from Britain. In fact, my early duties were given to me by Sandy who, as warden, was in the best position to know what the community needed. Later, his mailing system was merged with that at the Kiwi house and in the end we used anyone going to Baghdad who seemed remotely trustworthy. Australians and Irishmen were allowed to move between Kuwait and Iraq, and they also collected and delivered mail and provided us with newspapers and magazines from the embassies. These were photocopied and I helped to distribute them to people who were desperate for news. Sometimes they couldn't wait for delivery and would phone me and I would read them long passages from the papers and magazines.

There was a risk of being caught in possession of printed material from outside. The Iraqis were afraid that any circulation of such information would undermine their hold on the country. They were confiscating typewriters and photocopying machines to prevent such activities and also to stop the publication of underground newsletters. I used to stuff photocopied sheets down my jeans and hope for the best if I was stopped. Once or twice when I was at roadblocks they searched my handbag, but nothing more.

I once did a delivery job for the Kuwaitis. They got in touch with Sandy and he sent me to pick up a videotape of interviews they had conducted with some Westerners in hiding. They wanted it delivered to some French diplomats who were leaving with the evacuation of all French citizens in the country. I picked it up and, for want of a better place, stuffed it inside my pants. I was stopped at a number of checkpoints but although they looked in my car they never conducted a body search.

One of my biggest assignments came when Bob Morris asked me to pick up some food from a warehouse in Shuwaikh. It would be my longest journey and I jumped at the chance. The warehouse was owned by a Kuwaiti food importer who had some Australians working for him. I didn't know how much I was to collect; I was more concerned with what hazards I might come across on the way. I had every reason to worry. I ran into a checkpoint, and a soldier who was particularly difficult. He asked for documents in Arabic which I did not possess. He thought I was the wife of a Kuwaiti and detained me for ten minutes while he searched my car as well as my handbag. Because, early on, I could not bring myself to be more than curt with any soldiers I came across, my manner did not endear me to him. Later, I learned to be more conciliatory and chatty. The more scared I felt, the more I forced myself to smile.

The industrial area of Shuwaikh had been devastated. Shop windows were smashed, some of the stores had been burnt, litter was strewn everywhere, and vast areas had been damaged. The place was teeming with troops, army trucks and jeeps and there wasn't a woman in sight, which made me feel even more conspicuous. To make matters worse, I had been given the wrong directions and couldn't find the warehouse. I drove round and round for what seemed like ages, half expecting to be stopped by an army patrol. When eventually I found it, everything went smoothly. Two Australians and a Kuwaiti loaded nine boxes of frozen food, including hamburgers and potatoes, into my car. There was about sixty kilos in all. They moved fast. They were afraid the Iraqis would come storming in. They gave me a receipt although the payment had already been made by someone else. The Kuwaiti advised me that if I ran into trouble on my way back, I should bribe the soldiers with some of the food. It was common knowledge that the Iraqis were not getting enough to eat. After my experience on the way in, I expected the worst on the way back. As it happened, I drove the entire 20 kilometres without being stopped once. Back home I had the problem of where to store the frozen food, and I began phoning friends to ask if they had space in their freezers. Eoin finally found an empty one in the home of Canadian friends and we ferried the food round to them. I later learned the Iraqis had gone to the warehouse and raided it only minutes after I left.

I didn't always have to go so far for food; sometimes I found it in the vacated flats in my building after the occupants had left in a hurry. I called the German warden for permission to enter the flat occupied by my German neighbour, who had long since gone, and he told me to go ahead. I was able to replenish our stocks of toilet paper and toothpaste. But rummaging through other people's flats made me feel decidedly uncomfortable. I felt like a thief.

As my confidence grew I decided to visit the Sultan Centre supermarket in Salmiya. Before the invasion it had been the finest store in Kuwait. It was still open but many of the shelves were now empty or stacked with tissue paper. However, they still had a plentiful supply of frozen chicken, smoked salmon and fresh meat, though the queues were endless. If you arrived at 6 a.m. you could pick up a ticket number an hour later, so as to return at 9 a.m. in time for the opening at 9.30. The hassle was a big deterrent to going. When I mentioned the problem to Danuta, my Polish biochemist friend, she suggested I go with her. We would both wear white coats and jump the queue pretending to be doctors. We tried it and it worked without a hitch. When I finally got my false driving licence I felt even more confident and began visiting the street markets, at first with Eoin but later alone.

I became concerned about Ski, whom I hadn't heard from for some while and when Lima said she had some food for him from the resistance, but was scared to deliver it, I offered to do it for her. Ski was the only Westerner in his block and only went out to deposit his garbage. There were always people lingering around and I was afraid that if I was seen entering the building it would look suspicious and attract attention to him. On this occasion I picked up the food and delivered it to him without a problem, but on subsequent visits I made sure I wore a Kuwaiti dress and dark glasses, timing my visits for mid-afternoon when most people were taking a siesta. On that first visit I was shaken by his appearance. He had always been lean; now he was positively emaciated. He was never one to take much care in preparing his own food and seemed to like only powdered milk with an egg in it. From then on I made sure he got bread, powdered milk, cheese and vegetables, as well as cigarettes and books.

One day in early December Ski gave us all a terrible fright. We could get no answer from his phone. I tried several times. Diana, who lived nearby, was afraid to visit him but I asked her to check to see whether there were any army jeeps in front of his block. She reported back that there weren't, so I checked with Sandy to see whether he had heard of any Westerners having been picked up. But he knew of no new arrests. Neither did the American Embassy. So I decided to go to his flat, afraid that he might be sick, or even dead. There had already been a case of an Englishman discovered in his flat several days after he had died from a perforated ulcer. Tom Lemming, an ex-RAF-officer friend, said if Ski did not answer the door I should break it down.

'How?' I asked.

'Call the Iraqis. If he is sick he will have to be taken to hospital, anyway.'

I set out, worried about what I might find, and when I rang the bell there was no reply and no movement behind the door. I began banging and shouting his name. Then I heard a faint noise, and the door opened.

'Where on earth have you been?' I said. He looked at

me, mystified. He had not used the phone that morning and didn't know that it was out of order.

I was anxious to widen my community activities beyond food deliveries, mail collection and phone calls to my parishioners. When I heard that Lise, who was more fully involved in community service, was going to deliver mail to hostages held in Shuwaikh, I joined her. Most hostages were taken to Baghdad, but there were a number of small groups, captured in the early days of the invasion, who were being held at four different localities within Kuwait. Although one group lived under strict Iraqi supervision in prefabricated houses just outside Shuwaikh Port, they occasionally managed to make secret telephone calls. Some of them befriended their Iraqi guards and even had a few under their thumb. Lise told us how she had once taken a box of food to them. One of the Britons and his Iraqi guard were in the yard when she arrived. The Briton told the Iraqi: 'Run, Abdulla, run.' To her surprise, Abdulla obliged. He ran to the guard house and brought out a small table. Then, placing it beside the gate, he stood on it, took the food parcel and handed it to his prisoner.

On the day of my first visit Abdulla was not on duty and the mood was tense, one of the hostages told Lise on the phone. We arranged our visit for twelve noon when the guards were either praying or having lunch. It was a very quick transaction. Lise stopped her car at the gate. There were no guards around, only an overweight British hostage, who was running as fast as he could towards us. She passed him the mail, he gave her a handful of papers and was gone. These were a very touching few moments and the drama was written all over the Briton's face. He was panting, sweat was pouring off his forehead, as he ran, and his face was almost disfigured with the effort.

141

In November I visited other hostages at the Regency Palace, my first visit to the hotel since I said goodbye to Clem and George. I was to deliver a letter to an American, Myron Hanson, who was among seven Western hostages held at the time. This was not particularly hazardous: Eoin and Lise had done it before, although neither of them was comfortable about it. The hotel was under the control of the notorious Mukhabarat police. The soldiers on guard asked for my identification and then called the reception desk. Within minutes I was in the lobby. I had learned that to avoid arousing suspicion I had to look purposeful, speak loudly and sound confident.

I told the Iraqi behind the desk in the lobby that I had come to see Myron Hanson.

'Is he your husband?' he asked. I said he wasn't, but it made no difference. Myron came down.

He told me he was a library adviser and had previously worked at Kuwait University. The letter was from his parents and he was delighted. We then joined the other hostages who were sitting in the lobby. I did not recognise any of them but I discovered I had earlier spoken to one, Chris Protherby, on the phone before he was arrested. I expected them to be depressed but they were in quite an exuberant mood. The game was up for them, they said, and they were relieved to be out of it. This, I would find out later, was a common reaction among Westerners who had been detained after months in hiding. Clem, too, later told me how easily he came to terms with his arrest once he was at the Regency Palace Hotel.

I was to make one more visit to the Regency but this was a particularly sad occasion because among four detainees I was to see Richard Hattersley, the Jabriya warden with whom I had shared so much. I delivered toothbrushes, toothpaste and travelling bags to them. They were grateful for the things and they, too, sounded cheerful. A few days later, Baghdad announced the release of all hostages and the ones at the Regency were the first to leave Kuwait.

In late November I was asked by Hani Al Shaks, a Kuwaiti neighbour of Sandy's who had been helping foreigners, if I would be willing to shelter an American. I said I would. There were three empty flats in my building which the Iraqis had broken into and they were unlocked. I suggested he could use one of them and Hani came to check the place over.

'Who is this man, anyway?' I asked him.

'He is a priest,' he said.

I did not mind, though on the rare occasions I had met clergymen I was overcome by the fear that they would try to convert me or that I would blurt out something that would offend them. Three months before the invasion, I had not been keen to meet the pastor from the Seventh Day Adventist Church in Kuwait. But Clem's daughter, who belonged to the church and was visiting Kuwait, had brought him and his wife home once or twice. When I saw David Dunn I immediately recognised him as the Seventh Day Adventist pastor. We ended up getting on well.

David was already disillusioned. He told me when he arrived: 'You know, it's easy to be a Seventh Day Adventist. You are protected by your family, then you go to their school and then the church gets you a job. It's a safe little pond, but what a stinking pond it is.' He was disappointed with some of his flock. They had been avoiding him because he was an American. In one desperate effort to escape, he painted himself all over with a dark hair-dye so as to look like an Indian and be evacuated with the Indian contingent. The plan failed. At the last minute, the Indians, afraid that the Iraqis would see through his disguise, had had second thoughts. He had lived at the church which also served as his home. On Thanksgiving Day he had left the church for the first time and crossed the road to go to lunch at the home of David Prentice, one of four Britons in hiding there. While he was away, his church was raided, first by soldiers, later by thieves who stole $12,000 of church money.

A day after David's arrival, Eoin and I went to the church, which in fact was an ordinary villa in Salwa, to rescue some of David's possessions. There was a risk that someone might see us and report us for stealing, but we had been on similar missions before, and hardly gave it a second thought. I also had a special interest in going to the church: David had a Siamese kitten there and he promised it to me if I rescued it. I found it starving and miaowing incessantly. I had a job catching it. I subsequently fattened it up and named it Basil. He was beginning to thrive, until he encountered soldiers once again, this time at my flat.

XIX

It was not always easy to keep up the flagging spirits of those in hiding or even of those who were trying to help them. We all felt the allies were taking far too long to build up their forces in Saudi Arabia. It was October and still not certain that they would go to war, and no deadline for the Iraqi withdrawal had yet been set. The diplomatic shilly-shallying seemed to be going on and on; all we wanted was some kind of action. Some people still held out hope for an Iraqi withdrawal, but there were no signs of it. Indeed, they looked to be preparing for war. Not only had the number of Iraqi troops steadily grown, but they were placing field artillery pieces on top of the buildings along the coastline south of Kuwait City. Al Adan Hospital near the oil town of Ahmedi was declared a military hospital and a hundred beds, a quarter of the total, were set aside for victims of poisonous gas. Soldiers were all round my area and, two streets behind mine, they began digging deep defence trenches and bunkers. Iraqi commanders had received instructions to prepare for house-to-house fighting. If this happened, we were afraid we would be used as hostages, with troops moving into our flats and villas and shooting from there, using us residents as a shield. I thought that might be why they had not picked up all the Westerners. There could be tremendous bloodshed and we were all terrified of such a prospect.

About this time I heard some news which I thought I ought to pass on to London in a letter to Alan. It came

145

from Sandy, via an Iraqi resident in Kuwait whose cousin worked in the Iraqi Ministry of Defence in Baghdad and claimed to have access to confidential information. The Austrians were apparently sanction-busting by sending raw material such as alloys to Iraq which was using them in the manufacture of military hardware. The second thing was much more worrying. It seemed the Iraqis had a second nuclear reactor somewhere in the north of the country – it was generally presumed they possessed only one. This raised the spectre of a nuclear attack. Up to then, our main fear was the use of gas and the possibility that the Americans might respond to a gas attack with nuclear weapons. The reactor news suggested that the Iraqis could respond in kind, and that we would all be wiped out.

Nevertheless there was a sudden surge of hope that something was imminent and we were swept by a wave of optimism, as usual based predominantly on rumour. About the middle of October the French military attaché, Colonel Edouard Crespin, told me that he hoped something would happen in the next two weeks. He was the sixth person in two days to mention 'something' happening. There was Saddam's 'dream', for example, which was being widely quoted. In it, the Prophet Mohammed had asked him why he was waging war against a neighbour, when there was a real enemy that he should confront instead. The enemy was not named but was generally understood to mean Israel. The story was attributed to Baghdad Radio but I never met anyone who heard it broadcast. It did, however, give us some grounds to believe that Saddam might be preparing to withdraw.

There were other stories suggesting the pressure on those in hiding might be easing. Everyone had their own sources and, according to one of Ski's, Saddam had issued a decree to halt the sweeps to detain Westerners. This contradicted the facts. Two Britons living close to me in Salwa, and well-known to Sandy, had been picked up only two days before and were now at the Regency Palace, awaiting transport to Baghdad.

There was no sign of a let-up in the campaign of repression against Kuwaitis. On October 21 the Iraqis conducted a brutal raid on Mishref, south of the city across from Salwa. Not only did they pick up eight Britons and two Americans, they arrested a number of Kuwaiti army officers in hiding, dealing a severe blow to the resistance movement. It was not clear what prompted the raid, although there was one report that it was provoked by an attack by Kuwaiti resistance fighters on a detention camp in southern Iraq in which seventy Kuwaiti detainees were freed. Two days later I watched hundreds of soldiers surrounding the area. I was on my way home from talking to a Kuwaiti army officer who was in hiding, and everything was sealed off on the right of the road. I lived on the left and continued to watch the activity from my rooftop. The action went on for ten hours and Sandy was busy on the phone, reassuring Britons who were afraid they might be caught up in the sweep. The detention of Britons and Americans, and the arrest of Kuwaitis was a severe blow to the morale of everyone, especially to many Kuwaitis, who felt that, given the scale and severity of Iraqi reprisals, perhaps resistance was not worth the risk.

As new raids were reported in other places and checkpoints set up, the prevailing feeling was that the sooner the Americans launched an attack the better. In the absence of firm knowledge, the tendency was to invent good news and to set new deadlines for liberation. When we heard that Ali Majeed, one of Saddam Hussein's relatives, had been replaced as governor of Kuwait we thought that this might mean a let-up in the terror campaign. He had been responsible for the chemical attack on the Iraqi Kurds just before the end of the war with Iran.

All this suggested, to those wanting to believe it, a major development at the end of October: a withdrawal or an allied attack. There were other hints to support it, including an overheard telephone conversation between a Palestinian applying for a US visa and an Iraqi official who told him to wait until October 23 before making a decision. This coincided with rumours that the Iraqis would withdraw from Kuwait City and hand it over to the PLO. More significant seemed Bob Morris's discovery that two Iraqi generals and the Iraqi head of the civil administration had checked out of the Kuwait Sheraton and other officers were leaving the International Hotel. I thought most of it was wishful thinking and I told Bob so. There were no tangible signs from Baghdad to support any of the rumours and even Bob, who was desperate for some good news because he was depressed, acknowledged that the Iraqis had to rotate their forces.

I did not want to depress him further by telling him that I was not ready for the crisis to end yet. Despite my harrowing experience and regular bouts of anxiety, I was quite enjoying my life under occupation, especially as I was now being useful to others. It was as if I was living life on two levels: the real and the fictional. While I grappled with everyday problems, often getting angry and frustrated, there were times when I could distance myself and feel suddenly fascinated by it all. It was like stepping in and out of a novel or an adventure movie. Reality and fantasy sometimes overlapped, but it was the fantasy that often provided the missing pieces in the jigsaw and made sense of the crisis to me. I invented a role model to look up to. The outside danger forced me to listen to my inner-self more carefully. It tested my courage and

148

sapped my energy, but this, I thought, was just the situation to throw up heroes. The problems we faced brought out the best in some people and enabled us to get our values in the right order for once. Our new-found capacity to care and share and feel a sense of camaraderie overrode the racial divisions and self-centredness which had dominated our lives in the days before the invasion. We were going through a process of self-discovery that only a dramatic event like this could precipitate. I wanted it to continue. I was afraid that, if the curtain came down now, the heroes would be dragged off the stage before the end of the drama.

Almost everybody else wanted the crisis to end and to get back to their families. They weren't interested in extreme, life-enhancing experiences – they certainly weren't going to actively seek them out, as I did. Of course, having my Yugoslav passport made a great deal of difference. Only once did I feel seriously threatened as a Yugoslav.

One day in November I was weaving my way in my car through Salwa to avoid checkpoints, delivering stationery and bread to George Daher who was hiding in a villa 2 or 3 kilometres away. As I passed the Salwa police station, a white car outside pulled out and began to follow me. It had become my custom to look in my rear-view mirror in such situations, even before the invasion: following Western women was a favourite Kuwaiti habit. It had not happened since August 2. Now I was alarmed, especially when the driver overtook me and drove slowly in front of me. I pulled into the fast lane and caught up with him. We both stopped at the same time. I knew I had to be firm.

'What do you want?' I asked him aggressively.

'You are Yugoslav?' he said.

He spoke in fluent Serbo-Croat but said he was an Iraqi.

This is it, I thought. The Iraqis have found out who I am and that I am sending reports to London.

He went on talking. We had met in Belgrade, he said. He even gave the name of the place we were supposed to have met. I asked when this meeting had taken place but he became evasive and said it was while he was a student there. When he said: 'You can either come with me or I will come with you,' I did not know what to do, until I realised that the words were not spoken as orders. Then I realised he was just bored. He said he had nothing to do and asked for my phone number. I told him my phone had been cut off, but took his number to bring the conversation to an end.

I was now very near George's place but when I made a right-turn the Iraqi continued to follow, so I drove past the house and stopped again.

'What is it now?' I asked him. He had forgotten, he said, to ask me if I wanted to buy any cigarettes. I told him I didn't need any and he finally drove off. I drove round and round the block several times before daring to stop at George's house. The incident spoilt the day for me, but I never saw the Iraqi again.

On October 30 Saddam Hussein officially ordered his military commanders to prepare for street fighting. We had been hoping that, if war broke out, allied air power would be enough to eject the Iraqis and that the allies would leave Kuwait City intact. Commentators on the BBC and VOA seemed to contradict each other. Some predicted a war lasting a few weeks, others gave it six months. We became sceptical of military analysts. Meanwhile, troops began moving into abandoned villas and setting up gun emplacements.

November came with no withdrawal and no attack from the allies. All that happened was a toughening up by the Iraqis. They ordered everyone to register their cars and display Iraqi licence plates. There was a rush to the registration centres and queues of cars stretched for hundreds of metres, many of them staying overnight to make sure that they got their plates the next morning. For the most part, the Kuwaitis and Westerners ignored the order. But when the Iraqis announced in their local newspaper that only cars with Iraqi plates would be allowed petrol, some Kuwaitis began to register. Then everyone was ordered to obtain Iraqi identity papers. Non-Kuwaitis were told to report to the residence department by November 6.

I ignored all these orders. I was using forged documents anyway, including a forged Kuwaiti driving licence, and I was afraid that the Iraqis might discover my real identity. But, luckily, the Iraqis were the world's worst administrators. They were also corrupt. Each new rule was randomly enforced; it depended on who happened to be in charge, and whether he was open to bribery. He often was. The going rate for licence plates was a pair of Italian shoes, a Seiko watch or a portable cassette player.

Eoin went to the residence department to test the water. As a Canadian he was given a one-month visa which was due to expire on Christmas Day. When he later showed it at checkpoints, the soldiers were perplexed and still insisted on seeing his Kuwaiti driving licence. I found that reassuring, but the problem over residence permits plagued us until the end of the war. Though the Iraqis were incapable of enforcing the law, they still could not be depended upon to ignore it either. After Christmas, an Arab friend took my passport, and my Danish friend Lise's, to the residence department, asking for another month's stay. That, we decided, was all we needed. We were convinced that the war would begin before the end of January. When he came back with our passports, we discovered that, instead of residents permits, we had been given exit visas. Mine gave me a deadline to leave Iraq by January 13 — two days before the United Nations deadline for the unconditional withdrawal of Iraqi forces from Kuwait.

XX

It was all right for those back home. They had a much more rounded picture of what was going on in the world outside. We too were able to watch TV and listen to radio on the way things were developing, but our closeness to the violence around us made us more impatient for action. We could still hear the shooting at night, and growing numbers of Westerners were being picked up and sent away as hostages. Many of them had been betrayed by neighbours, former workmates and looters.

While Western leaders kept on condemning the invasion and demanding the withdrawal, Baghdad showed no signs of backing off. The UN Security Council was cobbling together one resolution after another, though haggling endlessly over the small-print. The mood among those in hiding was sombre. They felt they were only a tool in the hands of the big powers. 'We are hostages being used from three sides,' said Ski. 'The Iraqis are using us to prevent war, the Kuwaitis to invite war, and Bush might use us as a pretext to start war.' But we were stuck and there was nothing we could do about it. Perhaps it was this realisation that prompted the Westerners to begin laughing at their situation. The alternative to laughter was despair and despair was not an option we could afford.

If our days were to be numbered we resolved to indulge in whatever creature comforts we could lay our hands on. They were mostly gastronomic. Those who in the beginning had eaten nothing more imaginative than

153

baked beans, now began preparing quite sumptuous meals on their best china. Whoever was able to move around was invited. The liquor which came via Iraq flowed more freely than ever. Those with tennis courts and swimming pools ignored the dangers and began taking a dip or a game of doubles. Others went on to their rooftops and sunbathed to regain the tans they had lost in their basements. We even managed to wrench our talk away from politics, and humour returned.

We became glued to the BBC when it began broadcasting Gulf Link, with messages from those back home. Radio France International, the Voice of America, and the Australian and Canadian overseas networks began similar programmes. Two underground newsletters emerged. The *Kuwait Invasion Times* was produced by a group of Britons in hiding and the *Hostage Herald* by those I had visited who were being detained in Shuwaikh.

The violence outside might not have changed but our attitude did with the help of the ample food and drink we had acquired. We felt a certain shame in our relative affluence, especially as it was the Kuwaitis who were taking the brunt of the Iraqi repression. At one point Eoin MacDougald said to me: 'I feel like an impostor. The extent of our deprivation is shown by the demand for computer printing paper. People turn up their noses at meat unless it is Australian beef.' I wasn't feeling like an impostor. I was still worried about Clem; I had no idea of his whereabouts. I was constantly worried about thieves and being discovered by soldiers, and hardly a day went by without facing a checkpoint or hearing of an arrest. But there were certainly moments when I was able to let my hair down.

I knew something had changed when Bob Morris called and said: 'Choose a number, Jadranka. We are running a lottery.' Bob had been under great stress, living in a complex surrounded by soldiers and frequently looted by thieves. He also lived with an Irishman and an Australian who could move freely and took extraordinary risks in helping others but who Bob was afraid would draw attention to him. He was constantly worried the Iraqis would follow them home and uncover some twenty Britons and Americans who were hiding in the complex. His voice on the phone was usually strained and his mood despondent. But not this time. He asked me to choose a number between five and thirty. If the allies attacked on the day of the number I chose, I would scoop the pool. The stake was $10 on credit and the winner would stand drinks for all on liberation day. Sandy organised a similar sweepstake the next month. As it turned out we were all losers but at the time the lottery was a boost to our spirits.

I got an inkling of the luxury in which some Westerners lived when I first went to lunch with George Daher and his Polish friend Danuta. George sat in the garden by the swimming pool in a light-blue shirt and a dark-red tie. He was about fifty, his brown hair a little long and his face tanned and smiling. He looked like something out of *Country Life* magazine. He was a landscape architect and his garden had been artistically pruned. The trees were elegantly shaped and the orange trees were laden with fruit, while the rose bushes were flourishing.

He showed me the pump room next to the swimming pool where he hid. When the Iraqis came to the house, Danuta always managed to ward them off and they never made a search. Inside, the curtains were drawn and I could see thick Chinese carpets and beautiful lacquered furniture. He had an exercise room where he used to practise tennis volleys against a wall. The upper floor was just as elegant and spacious. While I was there, other visitors arrived, including a Polish architect and a Polish woman doctor and her Danish husband. We had an aperitif and then lunch. The dining table was beautifully laid with silver and crystal and there was a meal to match. It began with a vegetable soup and was followed by veal casserole and salad. The woman doctor had brought homemade bread and cucumbers she had pickled herself. There was no dessert but we had a choice of Cognac and Cointreau accompanied by coffee. I thought it was always the British who needed to keep up appearances, but here were others going to even greater extremes.

Soon after, I went to a lunch party at the Canadian ambassador's residence. He had gone and it had been taken over by a number of Canadians who had either been visiting Kuwait at the time of the invasion or were living there and had left their homes for the safety of the residence. The Iraqis had entered the premises in mid-September and since then it had been considered safe. There were about twenty-five guests enjoying a buffet lunch and a choice of five meat and fish dishes as well as salads and two desserts. One of the guests was Jean-Louis Pellerin, an accountant from Quebec who was compiling a bi-lingual invasion chronicle which he had entitled *The Last Grapefruit in Kuwait*. He boasted of being ⸁he owner of the only grapefruit left in the country. But Heinz, the German Canadian chef, proved him wrong and presented him with two fresh grapefruit. Jean-Louis vowed to mummify them so as to retain his claim. Heinz was a member of the Chaine des Rottiseurs and was preparing the menu for a post-liberation dinner. We asked what it would comprise. 'I've only worked out the hors d'œuvre – Brain à la Saddam. I have told our members to expect only a very small portion.'

Jean-Louis played his guitar and, flushed with liquor and full of food, we all had a sing-song. One Canadian who helped organise the party was suddenly stricken by guilt and begged me not to mention it in my despatches to London.

Not all expatriates in hiding lived like this. Two Britons living under water tanks on the roof of their ten-storey apartment block in Fahaheel survived in extreme discomfort. They fled to the roof after their flat was ransacked. They extended their phone line on to the roof and I occasionally spoke to one of them, Marshall Byiers, a high-spirited Scotsman, after Sandy said it would boost their morale to hear a woman's voice. Despite their hardship, they never complained, not even when it rained and their blankets got soaked. With a cookery book at his side Marshall used to toss pancakes over a gas stove under the Fahaheel sky. He was finally arrested in early December and detained at the Regency Palace where he told me, when I visited him there: 'Make no mistake. We lived really well.' He never succumbed to depression or self-pity and within days of our meeting he, along with all other hostages, was freed.

We all tried to keep up the customs of peacetime as if we were in our own countries. As Thanksgiving and Christmas approached, Sandy, who was an accomplished cook himself, decided to play a joke on Westerners who were busy looking for turkeys. He had already got hold of his from the Sultan Centre supermarket. The *Kuwait Invasion Times*, which poked fun at everything from the Gulk Link to Saddam Hussein, announced in its classified section that if anyone wanted a turkey he should contact General Schwarzkopf. Sandy sent a note round his parish confirming the advertisement. It read: 'The turkeys would be lightly greased with butter and fired from 16-inch guns from the US fleet in the Gulf. There would be no need to roast them, they will cook in flight.'

The BBC's Gulf Link was a marvellous idea. Not only did it keep us in touch with our friends and loved ones, but it gave us more than a few laughs. It began in the first half of September and I got my first message from Alan on September 26. It was not only wonderful to hear a familiar voice but his message sounded exactly as I'd expected. Delivered briskly in a soothing baritone, it told me everything I wanted to know: my letters were getting through, to keep on writing, we'd do the book together and my family was fine. I was pleased as punch. In mid-October I got a message from close friends in London, Susan Litherland and her husband Nasser. It was also nice because Alan and Susan were the only link with my sister in Italy and my parents in Belgrade. Such messages were a fantastic boost to our morale and, if I didn't get any, I would share in the pleasure of those of my friends who had. If no one had received any for a while, we would replay the recordings of those already sent. They all tended to be along the same lines. 'Keep your chin up, head down, think of you constantly, your mum is well but missing you. We all pray for your early return.' We began counting how many times the word 'constantly' was used. Some of the men amused themselves by putting physical characteristics and personalities to the women sending messages. 'I bet you she is fat and goes to church on Sunday,' was one comment I heard.

Several of the messages were sufficiently cryptic to intrigue idle minds. One came from the Woman in Red. There was no obvious reason, we thought, why anyone should conceal their identity – certainly not their first name. But the Woman in Red never revealed anything more about herself. Another message always began with what sounded like a sentence in code. 'To Marc with a C, hello, hello, what's the news?'

For want of anything better to do, some of the men phoned their friends to try to discover who the messages were for. In such a closely knit community it was hard to keep secrets. Eventually the inquiries revealed the messages were intended for two married men who had flirted with two women on the British Airways flight which was trapped in Kuwait on the morning of the invasion. When the women were released they made good use of the Gulf Link. The men were the subject of some envy, especially since they were getting messages from their wives as well. But after a while the Woman in Red and To Marc with a C disappeared from the airwaves. We wondered why!

XXI

The news came just after 3 p.m. on December 6. Iraq had announced that they would free all Westerners in Iraq and Kuwait. It was wonderful news, but it threatened to throw my life into disarray. We were all free to go — including Clem. He had smuggled out a letter to my sister in Turin and had also managed to phone Susan in London with a message she had passed on to me over the Gulf Link. I knew he was safe. When the news that we were free came over, I was sipping coffee with Tom Lemming in my flat. He was delighted. I felt somewhat less enthusiastic. While I was happy that we were all free and that all my new-found friends were able to go home, I still felt as though I might be robbed of the chance of seeing it all through to the end. I said something like: 'This is wonderful,' but I was aware what their departure would mean to me, left alone without the familiar phone calls and my delivery rounds. The absence of these duties would take much of the purpose out of my life. Not until later did the impact fully sink in. But I pushed it to the back of my mind and rushed round to Ski's and broke the news to him. He was not given to emotional display and merely said: 'Really?' He had suffered almost in silence while in hiding, though sometimes his face would show it. Apart from the odd food delivery he never took advantage of our community assistance network. He seemed quite self-sufficient and just wanted to protect his privacy and independence. He had never been part of the expatriate scene before the invasion and he continued to stay out of it, although I felt this might have been his loss. He had not heard from his wife since late August and I thought he would be eager to leave now that we were free to go. But he was not so sure.

Rose, an English girl with a Kuwaiti boyfriend, was in no doubt. She would definitely be staying and to prove it she invited me to their Christmas and New Year's Eve party. Not surprisingly, there was a general air of high spirits among all the Westerners, but I felt disconcerted and went to seek solace at Sandy's.

'I don't want to leave either,' he said. 'I, too, would rather see it through to the end.' But he was in a dilemma. His wife Barbara and their two sons were waiting for him in England, and Christmas was coming. He put off making a decision for the time being. He was like many others who were now torn between the friends they had made, and returning to their wives and families. I, too, had Clem in the back of my mind.

For two days after the announcement Westerners were advised to stay off the streets until it was clear that the Iraqis were going to keep to their word. But the prospect of freedom was too much for many and they ignored the advice. A party was arranged at Kiwi house but neither Sandy nor I was in party mood.

I decided to begin work on a story giving the reaction of the Westerners to their release. I was going to send it through one of them, and then I remembered they would all be back home to tell their own stories anyway. I watched them pass through different emotional phases after getting news of their release. First there was disbelief. George Daher thought Danuta was playing a bad joke when she told him about it. When he was finally convinced they both broke down in tears. Then there was euphoria. David Dunn ran down to tell me: 'When I get on that plane out of Baghdad, I'll just scream. The biggest

161

bonus is that the Iraqis aren't after me any more.' David Prentice, the British economist, congratulated himself on outlasting the Iraqis. 'Sticking it out in hiding was all I could do. I felt I won a small moral victory.'

Many by now were torn between staying and going. Anxious to get home, they also wanted to show their solidarity with the Kuwaitis who had helped them so much in so many ways. But they also wanted to survive the war we all now knew was inevitable. On the day of the news of their release, more than half of 350 Britons still in hiding asked wardens and the embassy for more information to help them make a decision. Many said they would not leave, and my hopes rose. But their wives and families were sending messages through the embassy, saying how much they were looking forward to being reunited. In the end only twenty-nine stayed on. Sandy was not one of them, much to my regret.

We had become good friends and it was a hard decision for him. He had close Kuwaiti friends and found it diffi- cult to explain his decision to them. He had spent ten years in Kuwait and during the crisis was a lynchpin of the British community. He had even compiled a register of Britons with expertise in all fields, in the belief that they would stay on until the end and be ready to help in the reconstruction of Kuwait. Judging from post-war events, their services would have been invaluable.

'I feel I am sneaking out through the back door,' Sandy told me. 'I feel cheated. We were waiting for the Ameri- can Stars and Stripes to come waving down the Fahaheel expressway.'

I still was.

While I quite understood why most people wanted to leave, it did not make me feel any better. I began calling friends to see who was going and who was staying. Tom Lemming was undecided, but tended towards leaving.

Eoin also had mixed feelings, but had a wife and two children in London.

I called Lise. 'Are you leaving?'

'Of course not,' she said.

When I spoke to Vladimir Dimitrijevic, a Yugoslav businessman who had been in Kuwait for nearly twenty years, I asked him the same question. 'The thought hasn't crossed my mind,' he replied.

It was Saturday afternoon, forty-eight hours after the Baghdad announcement, before the US and British told us it was now safe to leave our homes. The first evacuation flight organised by the Americans was due to leave the next day. Ski's phone was down again and I went to his flat to tell him about it. On the way, I dropped in at the Kiwi house and Lise and Eoin were waiting in the street with George Daher, who had Danuta's dog on a leash. As we stood in the middle of the road we watched men who had been in hiding for four months come out for the first time. Most of them wore T-shirts and shorts, and looked dishevelled and pale. Colin Wells and three other Britons walked towards us so slowly, they did not seem certain that it could all be true. Then we were all shaking hands and hugging each other. I saw Sandy walking briskly across a stretch of wasteground, seemingly oblivious to us. We called him over and there were more hugs. They had gone through so many ups and downs. Many of them had been holed up with each other for so long that they reminded me of old married couples who constantly bicker but never separate. Now all the squabbling was forgotten. Some hard times had bound them together.

One they would never forget was the tragedy that befell Bruce Duncan, the head of the British Army liaison team, who had managed to evade the Iraqis when they took thirty-five other members to Iraq soon after the invasion. A month before, the former British prime minister, Edward Heath, had managed to secure the release of Bruce's two teenage sons who were staying with him when the Iraqis invaded. The Iraqis were taking them to the airport when their army vehicle was involved in an accident. One son was killed and the other suffered a broken spine. When he was told, Bruce left his hiding place and wept at the hospital where his sons were taken. For some while it was not certain that the Iraqis would allow the dead boy to leave the country to be buried, and the British ambassador and the consul dug a grave in the embassy grounds. The Iraqis later relented and allowed his body and the injured son to leave the country. The blow to the expatriate community was profound and we all shared Bruce Duncan's grief.

Strong bonds were forged by hearing of little victories among others in hiding. Everyone applauded when one Briton escaped arrest by hiding under the bed, and there were more cheers when we heard about another who had been arrested in Kuwait, but who had managed to escape from Baghdad Airport to the German Embassy.

As they now all gathered to leave, I stood by, watching them talk excitedly. Was this the moment when all their camaraderie would begin to fade into memory? I was suddenly overcome by sadness. A verse from Kahlil Gibran's *Prophet*, which was my favourite reading during the occupation, came to mind: 'Shall the day of parting be the day of gathering?' Some did not leave for another three days but it was there in front of the Kiwi house that I mentally said goodbye to all my departing friends and to all those moments of fear and joy we had shared; to the life in which self-interest was permitted only in so far as it did not conflict with the well-being of the community.

Some of the most worthwhile experiences of my life were slipping into memory and, in an effort to cling on to them, I went with Ski and David to the Canadian residence and asked Jean-Louis to play his guitar once more. We even tried a verse of 'The House of the Rising Sun', but he kept hitting the wrong chords and I was missing the high notes. The show was over. That became even more obvious later in the evening when the three of us went to David Prentice's party. As soon as I walked into the room, I felt the magic had gone. It was a typical pre-invasion expatriate party and about the only difference was that the beer was branded and not home-brewed. The talk was of trivia. Someone said he would insist on taking his video recorder, whatever his baggage allowance. Another would not leave without his cat. The Britons planning to leave on the American flight the next day were being very secretive about it in case others heard and there were not enough seats. People who previously had been cowed were suddenly assertive, even cocky. The warden system had broken down and now everyone was making his own arrangements directly through the embassy. Some seemed to forget that Kuwait was still under occupation.

Sandy told me that two Britons and a Frenchman had banged on the door of an Iraqi woman and then abused her for causing them trouble. They were promptly arrested, although the Iraqis released them later. I stood in the room which was dimly lit and filled with smoke and, amid the babble of voices, I realised we no longer had anything to say to each other. I felt like an uncoupled railway coach, watching the rest of the train disappear into the distance. I left with David and we crossed the road to his church to see what was left of it. When we returned, Ski was standing by the car. He too was not in a party mood.

Eoin would tell me later that, even before they left Kuwait, those who survived the occupation behind closed curtains and barricaded doors were toasting their experiences and embellishing them freely. We had a taste of it when we spoke that evening to an American, a maintenance engineer at a Kuwaiti Hawk missile base at Sabah Al Salem, who we had heard had spent some time cramped up in an airconditioning duct in his flat with only his Yorkshire terrier for company. He told us he had been brought up by old China hands: 'Unfortunately a dying breed.' He was in ebullient mood and could not stop talking. He said on the first day of the invasion the Kuwaitis had destroyed forty Iraqi aircraft with the Hawk missiles. 'I myself saw three helicopters disintegrate in the air,' he said. He had spent twenty-three days in the airduct, living off dry spaghetti and water. At one point he had not left the duct for three consecutive days because the Iraqis kept coming back to loot his flat. They eventually took the water heaters, a bathroom basin and a kitchen sink. They returned every day, usually at the same time, which gave him a chance to come down, cook some rice and make phone calls before going up again. I couldn't understand why he had not asked for help. We could have moved him, as we had dozens of others. His explanation was: 'I am a loner.' He sounded like a masochist as well. He told us he had made a spear and would kill if need be. He was a very colourful storyteller but, like me, Ski was suspicious and we thought that truth might have got lost in the telling.

The credibility gaps were even more in evidence when the hostages returned home and told their stories. Distance is no respecter of facts. Eoin winced when he read some of the interviews given in the British press by people he had known well. Not only were they inflated accounts but they could have endangered those who stayed behind. We also cringed when we saw some of the television interviews with former hostages. In one they showed the faked documents they had been using. Back in Kuwait we were still using similar papers.

We now felt more vulnerable than ever. Our status was not clear. Few of us had any documents legitimising our presence and we also felt the Iraqis would step up their looting in flats, knowing they had been vacated by the hostages. With the departure of the American and British ambassadors and their staffs, we were losing our only direct link with the outside world. The deadline of January 15 was now looming and with it the almost definite prospect of war.

XXII

As soon as the release of the hostages was announced, I felt a thrill of excitement, thinking that Clem would soon be free, but it was temporarily overtaken by my disappointment at being parted from my friends. Now I looked forward to hearing from him. For weeks after he was taken to Baghdad I had heard nothing. My inquiries at the US Embassy led nowhere. In October VOA reported that fourteen American hostages in Baghdad had been freed, and I immediately called the embassy to ask if George and Clem were among them. They did not know, but promised to call me back. They didn't. The next day I called several times. The hostages had left Amman and were on their way to the United States. By now their names should have been released, but the embassy still kept putting me off. This was not good enough. I again picked up the phone, dialled the embassy number and demanded an answer.

'It is the Iraqis who are doing it, not us. We don't have the list of hostages. We just don't know.'

'If you don't know, find out,' I shouted. It did not go down well.

'Ma'am, we've serious problems here,' said the embassy man. 'We haven't had water or electricity since August 24.'

'I appreciate that you have problems,' I said. 'But we all have problems. I had problems when the Iraqis came and beat down our door and arrested us.'

Two hours later, Gale Rogers, the consul, called; Clem

and George were not among those released. They were being used as human shields at strategic sites, but she did not know where.

In early November my friend Susan came up with the message on Gulf Link saying that he was fine. Susan had also seen him on television. I was so relieved.

When Mohammed Ali went to Baghdad to try to get some of the hostages released, I felt confident that Clem would be among them because he was black. I again called the embassy to inquire and this time they read me an article on American law. They could not give any information to friends or next-of-kin without the prior consent of the hostage. I gave up, and concentrated on TV reports of hostages arriving in and out of Amman. I never saw Clem. Later I learned that George, but not Clem, had been one of those released.

It was very important to me to know that Clem was free, and I was surprised to find myself thinking of him with most tenderness when I recalled the moments he was not at his best. Not the fights, but the flaws. I now remembered them almost with fondness. Only once did I focus my mind on the good Clem, the generous, warm person who gave his all to the relationship. When I did that, I felt a searing pain and never tried again. The rest of the time my responses were spasmodic, a sudden flood of tears and a sense of desperation that would last only a few minutes. It usually happened when I remembered our last telephone conversation before he was taken from the Regency Palace. I still thought we were ill-suited and should go our separate ways. But to do that, he had to be free. I already was. I had a choice of either leaving or staying in Kuwait and had made it. If we were to separate I wanted us to start on an equal footing and he must have the same options as I had. The end of his ordeal should be the beginning of a new chapter in our lives.

He appeared, without warning, on my doorstep on the morning of December 10, almost three months after his arrest. He was ten kilos lighter, though fit and composed. He told me that he had been at Baghdad Airport when the first flight of evacuees arrived from Kuwait. When he discovered I was not on board, he was determined to get back to Kuwait. He went straight to the airline booking desk and bought a ticket for one of the regular flights maintained throughout the occupation. He needed only to show his Kuwaiti ID card. As the hostages boarded the planes for Britain and the United States, Clem was the only one going the other way.

I stood in the doorway, his arms around me and tears streaming down my face. There was a new bond between us, cemented by our harrowing experiences. I wanted to be with him and, as he began talking about his detention, I secretly hoped it might have trimmed his ego and modified his intimidating manner.

He had been held in four different detention centres, one of them, he thought, a chemical plant, although the Iraqis had called it a perfume factory. He had been treated well and was well-fed, although he had lost his appetite. He was sometimes taken on shopping trips, he told me, with other hostages to local towns. He was wearing an Iraqi suit and shoes bought on one of these shopping expeditions and paid for by the Iraqis. On these trips the Iraqis would clear the street of people, though the more curious would lurk around corners to get a glimpse of the hostages. They were allowed to make phone calls but only when the post office had been emptied of other people. Clem had also had dental treatment and some partial dentures had been made for him, but they were not a good fit and they hurt him. For a while he was detained at a 'model camp' where the Iraqis would bring the world press to show them how well the hostages were being treated. Once, he was approached by an Iraqi warden, who was a Christian, and asked whether he would do some propaganda broadcasts. Clem thought it was because he was black. We had expected this, convinced the Iraqis would try to exploit any grudges American blacks had against the whites. For all we knew, Clem was the only black detainee from Kuwait but, before he left for Baghdad, we both agreed he should resist any pressure to give public statements against his own country. Clem had had his share of trouble as a black man in the United States, but he wasn't the type to harbour bitterness. He refused to co-operate with the Iraqis and they did not press him.

He had had his bouts of depression. Table-tennis and Iraqi TV movies were not very good distractions. His only wish was to return to Kuwait to be with me and he wrote dozens of letters to the Iraqi authorities asking them to let him go back, if only for a visit. He wanted to make sure I was all right and, in his letters to the Iraqis, he argued that Kuwait was under their occupation anyway, so it did not matter whether he was a hostage there or in Iraq. When this ploy did not work, he went on hunger strike. When he failed to appear for breakfast and lunch one day, the Iraqis got worried and promptly sent doctors to talk to him. It was one of the wardens who left him in no doubt that it made little difference to the Iraqis whether he lived or died. Clem then returned to the dining room. But his efforts bore some fruit. On Thanksgiving Day they took him and others on a visit to another camp where he was reunited with George at a celebratory lunch. Even before his return from Baghdad, I felt his shortcomings would be his strengths in captivity, and so they were. The bottom line was that he was a robust personality, a Vietnam veteran and a survivor. In Iraq his initiative showed up well. He negotiated with the Iraqis to get better food and a video recorder for the hostages. The Iraqis recognised his qualities and sent him to cheer up a Frenchman who had become depressed. When the lone Japanese hostage at his camp applied for a transfer because he spoke no English, it was Clem who wrote his application, which was granted.

Just as Clem had come into his own in adverse circumstances while away from me, so too had I, away from him. When he was detained I was distraught, but I took hold of myself and had organised my own life without the rules he had prescribed. Things fell spontaneously into place for me, I began to function effectively. I was enjoying what I was doing and feeling quite proud of myself. Clem now noticed the change. He said he was proud of me. He could be as caring and generous as anyone when he wanted to. I was particularly touched that he had thought of bringing food for me from Baghdad, as well as cigarettes, although he didn't like my smoking. We sat holding hands and talking about all that had happened in the months since his arrest.

The joy of our reunion lasted only a few hours. In the evening we went to visit Sandy who had visitors, including a man with a twitch, who kept blinking. On the way home Clem accused me of eyeing the man. It was just like old times and the worst possible start to a discussion about the future of our relationship. The next day Clem was leaving for the States on an evacuation flight from Kuwait and I was staying on. It was to be our last evening together for what might be months. He wanted us to get married after the crisis was over and he asked for a commitment from me. I knew he loved me but, although I cared deeply, I was extremely uncertain. I suggested perhaps we should go our separate ways — though I didn't quite believe myself.

'I'll wait for you anyway,' he said.

We decided to make up our minds when I got out. It was a relief.

In January I got a message from Clem via a friend who picked it up from Baghdad. He still wanted to marry me. What I didn't know was that he sent it from his hospital bed. He had contracted hepatitis in Iraq but only discovered it on his return home.

XXIII

When the rest of the hostages left Kuwait, Ski stayed behind. It was a difficult decision for him and he agonised over it. While the evacuation flights were leaving, I would drop in on him on the way to the airport to see whether he needed a lift. He never did. IIe was torn between concern for his wife, with whom he had lost touch, and his job. He had written a comprehensive summing up of events and we were waiting to hear from Susan in London who was to try to get it published in the *New York Times*. He was also anxious to be available when the *Arab Times* finally began publishing again. Before the last evacuation flight out, he managed to place a call to Ikuko on the satellite and, satisfied that she was all right, he decided to stay on. I was pleased because I had an instinctive liking for Ski and great respect for him as a journalist.

Once the evacuations were over, I was planning to move from my flat; it would be too exposed and lonely. The idea of staying with Kuwaitis appealed to me. It was their country and I wanted to share some of their experiences to give me a different view of life from the one I'd seen so far. I also thought it would be safer to melt into a Kuwaiti neighbourhood and I had already been in touch with the Sultan family. Aziz's niece, Najat Sultan, had invited me to stay at her brother's house in Shuwaikh, which was unoccupied. There were other options as well. Danuta had invited me to move in with her, now that George had gone, and Lise was also willing to share a flat with me. Sandy had left me the keys of his house and there were several other flats available. I had a choice of a dozen places, but I couldn't make up my mind, and was waiting for something, or someone, to prod me in one direction or another.

Ski had a Kuwaiti friend called Osama, whom I knew slightly, and Osama said he had just the place for Ski and me. It seemed like an irresistible package, despite the danger. The house was occupied by a Kuwaiti and we could move in, but would have to stay in hiding. No going out, no phone calls, no visitors. Ski and I could work in the basement which was equipped with computers and a satellite telephone. The Kuwaiti and Osama would gather information for us and we could write our despatches and get them faxed by the satellite to major publications around the world. The Kuwaitis were watching the street and would give us advance warning if the Iraqis came. 'What do you think?' asked Ski. While I was a little concerned about losing my independence and contact with the outside world, the idea seemed too good to pass up. We were both willing to give it a try.

But I had some practical questions to put to Osama, such as what to do with my personal possessions and my car. He told me to store them with friends, but did not offer any help. 'What do I tell them?' I asked. 'Tell them you are going to Baghdad.' I had to just disappear and not let anyone know where I was. I knew that would be difficult, but I was so enthusiastic that I was prepared to do whatever it took. I knew that such plans came with some drawbacks and I could not expect to have it entirely my way. Besides, I trusted Ski's judgement and he was already packed and ready to move.

Osama said he would give us a weapon to ward off any looters — an iron bar! It did not sound reassuring but I

175

reckoned that I was already facing risks anyway. On the advice of friends, I had kept a baseball bat at home and an iron rod in the car – though I didn't know whether I would be able to defend myself with them if the time came.

Osama insisted he and his friend were very security conscious, but stressed that, if the Iraqis caught us, we could be executed as spies. This was no surprise to me. I had already discussed it with Ski. I was ready to accept the risk without hesitation, partly because I was already operating with forged papers and sending reports to Britain.

I was extremely unwilling to think about death. Since the invasion I had been preparing for arrest, rape and a confrontation with looters. These, I felt, were manageable problems. Death, however, was final, so what, I reasoned, was the point of preparing for it. How do you prepare for it, anyway? The only way I could think of was to consider all the monstrous ways it could happen. Once or twice I had a fleeting image of my body lying in a pool of blood. That was too frightening so I blotted it out. Thinking about death was defeatist and destructive. Besides, I was convinced I would survive. There were times I even felt invincible. I knew the risk was there, but what's life without risks? Not much, I thought. Without this attitude I would not have been able to continue gathering information and sending it out. Most of my colleagues on the *Arab Times* had left, or were waiting to leave the country. Those who stayed did not dare dabble in journalism and reporters from the international press, such as the *Financial Times*, the *Washington Post* and Dutch Radio – who were all in the country at the time of the invasion – had managed to escape.

I began gathering information on August 2 and never once stopped until I left the country on March 10. The effort required a lot of planning and caution to avoid unnecessary risks. While in hiding, I got information over the phone. We were afraid that the phones might be tapped and although I was prepared to take the risk, some of my contacts were not. I still managed to develop a sizeable network of contacts, covering about a dozen neighbourhoods. I would jot down the main points of all my conversations and organised them later in my hand-written diary, which also included descriptions of my thoughts and feelings, and of those around me. I used Clem's computer to write my letters because I had sent my own for safe-keeping with a Palestinian neighbour. When Clem left the country I hid it, together with the early volumes of my diary and my British passport, in the space above the ceiling that housed the airconditioning units. When I suspected my flat might be looted, I packed Clem's computer and took it to Sandy's house. For a while, I used a friend's typewriter, but then the Iraqis began seizing typewriters. All my letters from January onwards were handwritten.

Once the hostages were allowed to leave, I got my letters out with them, but, before their release, I used Sandy's mail route via Baghdad and Amman. Sandy also arranged for us to receive letters and messages from Britain by the same route. The letters would arrive on a disc and were printed out by Sandy and distributed by Eoin, me and other 'postmen'. This was quite an efficient system but occasionally it gave us problems. We were puzzled by one letter on the disc from a girl who was ultra security conscious. It was simply addressed: To my Brother. Sandy searched for the name of the sender for clues. The letter ended only with: Your Loving Sister. But a few phone calls solved the mystery and it was duly delivered.

From October, we also used the British Embassy in

Baghdad to forward letters on to Britain. Trust was an elusive quality in those days and Sandy had to choose our 'postmen' carefully. We were also worried about reports that the Iraqis were both confiscating letters and censoring them. When I heard one of the evacuation flights was leaving from Basra instead of Kuwait, I avoided sending a letter on it, afraid the evacuees would be searched. Only when I discovered that the flight had been diverted, because of a resistance attack on an Iraqi plane at Kuwait Airport, did I give it to one of the passengers.

After the hostages had gone, we were cut off with only a few satellite phones linked up to fax machines. To my knowledge there were only three such phones in Kuwaiti hands and, in late December, we learnt that one of those had been stolen. They were frequently moved from one place to another to keep them away from the Iraqis.

While in Salwa I arranged with Hani Al Shaks, who had access to the phones, to have my stories sent to Sandy's fax number in Milton Keynes. His was the only fax number I knew. I got one message across on January 10, but I suddenly had to leave Salwa and move 20 kilometres away, to the home of Dr Aziz Sultan in Shuwaikh. Since late October, I had been visiting him every Friday, together with his other Kuwaiti and Western friends. Once the air war began, few of us ventured out and this seemed the end of my correspondence with London. But Aziz came to my aid. He introduced me to a Kuwaiti friend who had a phone and was willing to relay my letters. But I could not continually use the same phone and so I again turned to Hani for help. He still had access to a phone, he said, but I would have to get the story to him. Aziz, who despite the air war continued to travel daily to Mishref to spend nights with his brothers, agreed to meet Hani at the Mishref mosque. Hani cycled to the rendezvous point, took the story from Aziz, and had it sent on. I never asked how.

On February 3 I gave a letter to Aziz's Kuwaiti friend but only much later did I learn that it never left Kuwait. It was on February 6 that the phones inside Kuwait were cut off for the first time. This was a major setback. While I could still gather information from neighbours, and visitors, and from Aziz, who was making daily trips to other areas, I was unable to send any letters. It was a journalist's nightmare; getting information but being unable to pass it on.

On February 21, three days before the ground war began, I decided to take a letter myself to Hani. I knew the chances of him being able to send it were slim, but I had to try. I paid a Syrian who was supplying us with cigarettes and vegetables, to take me in his car to Salwa. I was going out for the first time in forty-one days. The day before, I had sent the driver to check the route for safety. He reported all was clear. I donned my abaya and the trip went without a hitch. Hani was willing to try to get my letter out, but he could make no promises: the Iraqis had begun rounding up Kuwaitis to take to Iraq in the event of a ground war and he dared not go out. That letter, too, never left Kuwait.

I had never thought I would be able to get all my letters out, anyway. But it was important for me to try. Of twenty-one letters I sent to Alan in England, only the last three failed to arrive. Given the conditions we lived in, it was no small feat. I could not have achieved it without the help of dozens of people, some of whom I had never even met.

XXIV

As the Western alliance took shape outside, the Westerners and the Kuwaitis became similarly bonded inside. Although the victims of atrocity and deprivation, the Kuwaitis often took great risks to help Westerners who were suffering. They risked having their houses destroyed, and even threats of execution, by giving shelter to expatriates. They supplied them with food and organised a distribution of money. While some thought it was in the Kuwaitis' interest to help Westerners survive in the country – as a lever for ensuring Western support outside – it had also become clear that the help they gave was often as spontaneous as it was generous. If the help appeared to be generally one-sided – I heard of no expatriates taking part in the resistance – the gains were not always one way. Some Kuwaitis were happy to allow their vacated homes to be occupied by Westerners to keep looters at bay.

The Westerners were of great propaganda value. They were writing huge numbers of letters to their families back home which were being widely reported in the Western press and attracted more publicity about the plight of Kuwait than the Kuwaitis could ever have done. Many of the accounts of atrocities and devastation first came to the attention of Western governments as a result of information from expatriates.

In early October I realised that most of my contacts were still foreigners, including non-Kuwaiti Arabs. I was anxious to talk to Kuwaitis at first-hand about their own experiences, and their hopes for the future. I picked up the phone. After two hours I had managed to locate only one Kuwaiti acquaintance, Faisal Al Manai of the Kuwait Hotels Company which owned the International Hotel and the Khairan resort. He was preparing to leave. His hotel had been seized by the Iraqi army command and then bombed by the resistance. Khairan had been occupied and he lived in an area which was a staging post for Iraqi troop movements. His family were in Egypt and within days of my talking to him, he had managed to escape to join them.

Many of the Kuwaitis I knew had either left the country or moved house, and their offices were shut down. The only way to meet them was by word of mouth, put out along the chain of contacts beginning with expatriate friends. Jerzy, a Polish architect, put me in touch with Ali Al Badr who worked at the Gulf Bank. Bob Morris introduced me to Dr Jawad Behbehani of the Dental Centre. I also got to know Aziz, who came to my building with a letter to be mailed. He rang my bell by accident and when I asked if he would be willing to talk to me, he agreed. I was not to know it then, but it was the beginning of an association which led to my hiding out in his house right through the war and the liberation. I began visiting his house on Fridays, and it was there that I met a number of Kuwaiti women. There was Aziz's niece Najat, along with two other Kuwaitis, Leila Al Qadi and Haya Al Mughni. I also renewed an old acquaintance with Dr Ahmed Bishara, a professor of engineering at Kuwait University. He was in the United States when the Iraqis invaded but he made his way back to Kuwait across the desert two weeks later. During my Friday talks with the Kuwaitis, I began getting an insight into what they were doing and what their expectations were for the future.

The invasion had triggered a process of self-examination among many Kuwaitis, who were well aware of the country's political and social shortcomings but, until then, had felt impotent, or too complacent, to change them. The invasion set in motion a sudden political awareness which spread rapidly among those who stayed behind in Kuwait. The more they suffered under the Iraqis, the more vocal the Kuwaitis became about their vision of their country after the liberation. They felt they had earned their place in the decision-making process and were determined to make their voices heard. They were united in their desire for democratic government and were not impressed by promises from Taif, where the royal family was in exile, about the reinstatement of parliament; they did not trust the Al Sabahs.

After the Amir dissolved the National Assembly in 1986, the government used force to quell demands, in the year leading up to the invasion, for a return to the 1962 constitution. This guaranteed the continuation of the Al Sabahs as the ruling family, but it more clearly defined its powers, leaving the legislature in the hands of an elected parliament (though the executive powers remained with the royal family, which effectively controlled the government). An interim National Council, set up just before the invasion, was not considered to be even a step in the right direction by many Kuwaitis. They thought it was a poor substitute for a proper parliament and that the government was stalling. The opposition, which was grouped around thirty former deputies, went so far as to describe it as an insult to people's intelligence. Angered, they defied orders not to assemble and continued to meet at their traditional gatherings, the diwaniyas, to air their grievances. Many of them were arrested, although no charges were pressed and they were later released. They boycotted elections for the

National Council in June, which threw up names that would hardly have qualified for any *Who's Who* in Kuwait. They were an unusual mix and included bedouins and businessmen, teachers and shopkeepers. They also contained a religious element and were a widely disparate group. The one thing they had in common was that they had no links with the ruling family, nor the merchant families: these had been the two prerequisites for having a voice in how the country was run previously. As it turned out, the Council, with its twenty-five appointed and fifty elected members, had no time to deal with the issue of parliament. Its first task was to be the problem of Saddam Hussein.

On the day of the invasion, while most Kuwaitis were still trying to discover what had befallen them, members of the new National Council fled to safety in Saudi Arabia on the coat-tails of the royal family and the government. The invasion also came while many leading Kuwaitis, and, to be fair, members of the opposition, were vacationing out of the country. One Kuwaiti told me: 'Our problem is our politicians are only part-timers.'

As the occupation went on, and the feeling of solidarity among all levels of Kuwaiti society grew, so did the awareness of the inadequacies of the rulers and the defects of the poorly organised opposition. This realisation increased the commitment to change the system when liberation came. The Iraqis also gave the Kuwaitis practice in suffering. 'There is nothing the Al Sabahs can do to us now that the Iraqis have not already done,' Dr Bishara told me.

Much of my discussion with Kuwaitis centred on whether they would be able to reduce their reliance on foreign labour and instead do the work themselves. Kuwaitis were well-known for their opulent and often indolent lifestyles and, during the occupation, some got their first taste of manual labour. With the breakdown of public services and shortages of food, they began collecting their own garbage, growing vegetables and baking bread, some even became barbers. So did that mean they would adopt a new work-ethic? A young Kuwaiti from the Al Houti family, who got a job in the public administration only days before the invasion, was cynical about the prospect. 'People don't change overnight. Within six months of the liberation we'll be back to square one. Wasta [use of influence] will be rampant, the housemaids will be back, and people with influence will again get away with their crimes.' Others were more optimistic and even thought that the invasion was a blessing in disguise, acting as a catalyst for change. Dr Jawad Behbehani said: 'If we don't come out of this experience purified and clear-headed, we shall have no future.'

Important though the future was, the present had still to be lived through. Most of the talk was about Iraqi brutality, but the stories of atrocities were often greeted with some scepticism, as they were in the West. Some Kuwaitis believed the government in exile was exaggerating reports to force its Western allies to act more swiftly. Rumours spread like the plague in Kuwait and stories of events that were bad enough were often made to sound worse as they were passed on. Reports of Iraqi cruelty were often impossible to verify without putting your own life in danger, but many Kuwaitis I knew took great care to check accounts for accuracy. Aziz Sultan was one of them, and I did my best to follow his example. Early in February, he told me of two teenage boys who had been shot in Kheifan. On the day after the Iraqis fled, I visited the place and saw the bloodstains on the wall. It turned my stomach, but at least I had confirmed it.

Another reliable source was Hani Al Shaks. He had been educated in the United States and worked for an investment company. He was of great help to Westerners in hiding, providing them with food and moving them to safe-houses if they were in danger of arrest. He also salvaged their possessions if they were arrested. He had been caught and beaten up by the Iraqis. When they devalued the Kuwaiti dinar and inflated the Iraqi currency, Hani took an extraordinary risk. He stood in front of a local Co-op approaching Kuwaitis and offering them 10 Iraqi dinars for every Kuwaiti one – twice the black market value. It was his way of undermining the Iraqi economy. Possession of Kuwaiti dinars was an offence at the time and only banks were authorised to exchange them. Other Kuwaitis were doing the same as Hani and soon the bottom fell out of the market. I think Hani may have been involved in the resistance movement; he had unusually detailed information about raids on the suburb of Rumaithiya which was a known hotbed of the resistance and where public executions took place. But in those days our motto was: the less said, the better.

I never saw any atrocities, and reports reaching me were often third-hand. They originated from families and neighbours of those killed, who described how they were forced to watch, which was a practice that the Iraqis used as a deterrent. Danuta told me she had seen the bodies of a mother and her two children, aged six and eight, who had been brought to the Adan Hospital where she worked. They had been shot in front of a Co-op because the children became bored with queuing for food and began singing; one of the songs was the Kuwaiti national anthem.

Some of the stories of executions were so sickening, it was easier not to believe them, although they were so widely reported it was difficult not to. One way of executing resistance fighters was by crucifixion. To try to force one Kuwaiti to inform on the resistance, the Iraqis took him to a house and showed him four resistance fighters nailed on the wall. He was so overcome he told the Iraqis what they wanted to know, and when he related the story to my friend, the Polish doctor, he wept uncontrollably with shame. Another story concerned a member of a well-established Kuwaiti family of Iranian origin who was shot and then crucified with nails through his eyes.

The weekend was the favoured time for executions. A letter I wrote on November 20 described the atmosphere at the time: 'It is Friday. By now the execution squad sent weekly from Baghdad must have arrived and detainees will be waiting on death row for Saturday, the execution day. The dead are usually dumped in front of their homes from moving vehicles. Two Saturdays ago, the mother of a Kuwaiti teenager, her face alight with relief at the sight of her son who had disappeared weeks before, opened her arms to receive him at the garden gate. He took a few steps and fell lifeless into her arms — shot dead by a bullet in the back.

'When Salim's brother failed to return home one night in early November, he went looking for him. All he found was his brother's car. Two days later, a strange odour made him open the boot. There lay his brother, blood caked on his disfigured face. Some 3,700 Kuwaitis have been killed since the invasion, not including those who died in early fighting. More than 8,000 detainees could meet with the same fate.

'But for some Kuwaitis there are worse things than death. They speak of a missing compatriot who one night appeared in a torn and stained dishdasha at a suburban diwaniya. He had a vacant look on his face and could not tell his name or address. He answered each question with: "Ana ahabek Saddam." (I love Saddam.) He had been in detention from the beginning of the invasion. The man may never regain his sanity.'

Most of the atrocities and killings were inflicted upon people suspected of being in the resistance movement, although many who were not involved suffered too. Although led by police and army officers, many resistance fighters were high-spirited teenagers who went on Rambo-style night raids hunting Iraqis. Some mounted suicide missions on Iraqi trucks carrying troops. One of their problems was shortage of weapons. And this was one reason why the Kuwaiti army failed to put up much of a fight on the day of the invasion: they were short of ammunition, which had been hidden in places known only to a selected few. The resistance fighters had to find their own, and many took advantage of the low morale among the Iraqi soldiers, who sold them rifles for about $144 each. Some were even reported to have bought tanks for $18,000 each and then blown them up.

When news of Iraqi reprisals leaked out, the Prime Minister in Taif called on the resistance fighters to lay down their arms and resist passively, to stop further bloodshed. But within a few days they fired a missile at an Iraqi aircraft taking off from Kuwait Airport. It failed to bring the aircraft down, but it did have a demoralising effect on the Iraqis, as did the explosion at the International Hotel in which three Iraqis were killed. After the raid at Mishref the resistance's activities were curtailed, but did not stop. They changed their tactics and began blowing up cars at places frequented by Iraqis. On November 15 an explosion ripped across the Suleibikhat roundabout, which had become a bus terminal for soldiers travelling home. Ten people, not all Iraqis, were killed.

The Iraqis continued their campaign of reprisals against Kuwaitis until the day they withdrew. Although they captured many who were 'guilty' of involvement in the resistance, many innocent Kuwaitis also fell victim. One of them was Fayez Marzouk, a municipality engineer who had spent two weeks in detention in one of the police stations. I met him in mid-October through Elisabeth Nowacka, my Polish doctor friend. She saw Fayez being taken away by the soldiers after an Iraqi woman neighbour, in Sabah Al Salem apartment block where they all lived, accused him of being an Al Sabah sympathiser. Fayez told me that interrogation and torture were always carried out at night. He was repeatedly hit on the head with a rifle and was made to walk slowly through lines of soldiers who each slapped him on the face. He was also forced to urinate on the Kuwaiti flag, clean a lavatory pan with it and then wipe his face on it. For weeks after his release he said he was haunted by the screams of other inmates who were subjected to severe beatings and electrical shocks. After release, Fayez often sought solace in drink. He called it a Saddam drink.

An even more harrowing story I heard from Hani's cousin Ali, a twenty-six-year-old Kuwait Oil Company mechanic who had spent four and a half months in detention, during which he was subjected to repeated interrogation and torture. I met him two weeks after his release on December 20 and, as a safety precaution, we split the interview into two two-hour sessions at two different locations. He spoke in a level voice, but his face was tense and his hands were never at rest. Even more distressing than his descriptions of torture was the fact that the Iraqis were slowly and cruelly trying to break a man who was innocent of what he was accused. Day after day, week after week, he suffered beatings, electrical shocks and mock executions. I understood why, in the end, he lost all will to live. Just listening to him made me feel drained.

Ali was captured on August 3 at the 15th Brigade Headquarters, where he had gone to join the army as a volunteer. Over the next three months he was dragged from one Iraqi camp to another, about ten in all, with several hundred other Kuwaiti civilians, aged between thirteen and seventy. They were questioned, pressured to become informers in return for freedom, given food that barely kept them alive, and had no toilet facilities. At one point, the detainees shared two rooms in a Basra prison that Ali said were designed for 100 prisoners but were now crowded with 400. They all had to squeeze into one room, and use the other as a toilet. By the time they left the camp more than a month later, the human excrement in the room was knee-deep and the indescribable stench made prisoners vomit.

Ali was released on October 30 but that same night he was re-arrested and accused of helping the resistance. When he explained he had just been released from detention in Iraq and gave the name of an Iraqi officer who could confirm it, he was accused of bribing him. He spent fifty days blindfolded and handcuffed, and nights in torture chambers in three different detention centres in Kuwait. On one day he was beaten with sticks from 1 a.m. until breakfast-time with only short intervals between beatings. He was also given electrical shocks on his temples and genitals and was one night invited to make his last request, as his torturer loaded a pistol. Instead of pulling the trigger, he punched him and when Ali fainted, he poured water over his head to revive him. He was then tortured all over again. He was finally freed when a Kuwaiti neighbour who had named Ali as a resistance fighter – while himself under torture – repented and admitted he had been lying.

I had lots to report to the outside world but because of my exposed position since the evacuation of the other hostages, I needed a safe-house where I could work and feel secure. The place Osama had found for Ski and me seemed to be the answer. Ski moved into it on December 11. I was to follow in a couple of days, when I had sorted out my possessions. The next day, early in the evening, Ski phoned. I was a little surprised. This was against the rules that Osama had laid down. Ski could not talk long but he said he was not sure the house was secure. He gave me no details but said, 'It is too deep.' He advised me to wait a couple of days before I moved in. I was baffled. Later that evening, he called again. He was back at his own flat. I jumped into the car and went to see him. He had left, he told me, because there was too little security to justify the risk. In the twenty-four hours that he had spent in the house, the Iraqi census people had come and knocked on the door on two occasions, and he had had no warning of their arrival. The Kuwaiti who lived in the house was never there, the basement was crammed with all kinds of sophisticated electronic equipment that could incriminate us, and the bathroom basin was black with the ashes of burnt papers. Later, Osama told him it was bad luck the Iraqis had come that day but Ski was not to be persuaded. 'Journalism is one thing, spying is another,' he told me. I understood. If we were going to risk being shot as spies we could not settle for security arrangements inadequate even for journalists.

A few days later, after learning that his story had not appeared in the *New York Times*, Ski left Kuwait. His advice to me before his departure was to keep a low profile, hide my notes, and use code words to write my diary. 'Stick with foreigners; let the Iraqis believe you are one of those eccentric, crazy foreigners,' he said. The way I felt about my immediate future as I said goodbye to him at Kuwait Airport made me wonder whether he wasn't closer to the truth than he thought. Had I bitten off more than I could chew; was I indeed going crazy?

XXV

Because of Kuwait's wealth, the plunder was on a scale unprecedented for a state of its size. Anything from civil airliners and construction cranes to refrigerators and kitchen sinks were up for grabs, to say nothing of the gold from the souk and the bullion in the bank vaults. The Iraqis themselves made examples of several soldiers caught stealing, and shot them. But there was little doubt in most people's minds that the booty was Saddam Hussein's reward to his conquering army. The looting continued from the day of the invasion to the night of February 25 when the Iraqis fled the city, taking with them anything they could fit on a truck, bus or jeep. Those fleeing on foot carried what they could grab in bags. When allied aircraft attacked the fleeing army on its way to the border, the road and the surrounding desert were strewn with both corpses and what they had taken with them. There were stolen cars and other vehicles and a wide range of other valuables.

The looting took place on three levels. On an official level, the Iraqis systematically removed public property from banks, government offices, and Kuwait Airways airliners, as well as what they could find of the wealth of the Al Sabah and big merchant families. In some cases they transported away entire factories. They took sophisticated medical equipment and supplies from hospitals, office furniture and computers, and construction equipment. They were transported by the Iraqi army trucks and big transporter vehicles, some of them from Jordan.

In late August I watched from my flat as army trucks carried away luxury yachts and cruisers stolen from marinas and sea clubs which dotted the coastline. Each carried two boats and towed a third. I counted more than twenty, all similarly loaded.

On the second level, groups of soldiers prowled the city and its suburbs, taking any cars that took their fancy and breaking into empty flats and villas, stripping them bare of contents. These were the entrepreneurial thieves who had even brought trucks and Sudanese labourers from Iraq to help them ship the loot back home. People with gold and jewellery in bank safe-deposit boxes often had to share it with Iraqis guarding the vaults to recover any of it. Searches for Westerners, weapons, or resistance fighters nearly always resulted in theft as well. The officers stole almost anything that caught their eye, though they particularly went for video recorders, hi-fi systems and TV sets. Gold and cars, however, were at the very top of the theft list. One Kuwaiti businessman never gave up hope of recovering his stolen Mercedes. When he spotted it parked in front of a supermarket one day, he pulled out his spare keys and drove it home. Only then did he open the boot to discover it was crammed with gold bars. Not everyone was so lucky. One woman who tried to hide her jewellery from soldiers searching her home, dropped it in a pot of boiling water. The officer in charge of the search came in to the kitchen and remarked that he could smell something good cooking. He lifted the lid on the pot where the jewels were boiling and remarked: 'So that's what you eat in Kuwait.' He took them with him.

The third category of thieves were mainly Arab and Asian expatriates who saw an opportunity for easy pickings. They had the advantage of knowing the areas and the people who lived there. But they had to be careful to avoid the soldiers, who resented the competition and who even fought each other over the spoils of war.

Few were immune from the thieves. Indian women had gold chains snatched from their necks, two Britons were tied up by soldiers who broke into their flat and then looted it for four hours, finally leaving the Britons unharmed. A Palestinian gave a lift to two soldiers and when they arrived at their stated destination they ordered him to get out and give them his car keys. The Palestinian walked home. We all saw the thieves at work. When they were soldiers, we tended to look the other way.

The area where I lived was fertile ground for theft, being at the very end of Salwa with little passing traffic. Sometimes a whole day would pass without a single car on our street. Of twenty-five houses, about a third were still under construction and only four were occupied; the owners were either on holiday at the time of the invasion or were quick to flee the country.

The vultures descended early, taking away the contents at night in pick-up trucks. But as the soldiers rotated, their successors came to try their luck as well. I couldn't imagine that our area had anything left to steal, but it did not stop them from coming time and again. One small prefabricated house in the next street about 30 metres away from my building was looted at least six times.

One day, I watched two soldiers emerge with loot wrapped up in what looked like tablecloths. Having swung the bundles over their shoulders, they walked slowly along the sandy stretch by the wall, looking furtively around them and not daring to step on the road.

My first direct experience of theft, not counting the visit by Captain Iyad and his men after our arrest, came in the middle of September when a truck belonging to our neighbour disappeared. The next night the wheels of another went too. And the next, the wheels of two cars. They would have taken the cars themselves, if they could have started the engines. With thieves and soldiers hovering around the area, I lived for months in virtual silence, until one morning in early November I said to myself: 'To hell with everything!' I put on a tape of Italian opera sung by Mario del Monaco and threw open the windows. In the 1950s and even 1960s he used to be one of the world's best tenors and, now, when I turned up the volume to the maximum, his voice and the music were an absolute delight. The Italian opera had an enormously revitalising effect on me and, together with the verses of Kahlil Gibran, gave me a fresh zest for life. I remembered the words of Leonard Bernstein, who described music as an experience that does not have to pass through the sensors of the brain or be considered in the mind. He called it a 'direct hit', and now, more than ever before, I knew what he meant. Exhilarated, I called Sandy to share my excitement with him. 'Sandy, I feel so strong, I can take on the entire Iraqi Army.'

As I spoke, I looked out of the window and to my consternation saw some twenty soldiers pour out of four cars and a tow-truck in front of my building. I rushed down to meet them. They made no bones about what they were after. There were four cars outside, including mine. I told them not to take mine, and they agreed, but only managed to take two of the others. One wouldn't start.

I perceived my biggest threat from thieves when a large group of soldiers moved into a derelict villa across some open ground from my block in the middle of November. I asked Zeinab and her husband what to do about it and they suggested I call the police. They gave me the number of the city police headquarters and when I got through, it was answered by a senior officer.

It turned out to be Colonel Hashim, the chief of Iraqi police in Kuwait City. He listened patiently to what I had to say and then promised to come in person to check out my fears. I was afraid that he might come up to the flat, so I hid all traces of Clem, my diary and video camera. I changed into a kaftan-type dress and prepared a story to tell him if he questioned me. Three hours later at 1 a.m. he phoned to say he could not find my home. I suggested he leave it till next morning but he would not hear of it. 'The soldiers might run away by then,' he said. 'We are coming now, please come out on your balcony and wave to us.'

He arrived with about twenty uniformed and armed men. They stood in front of my gate until I came down. The colonel was a short, handsome man of about forty with fine features. He spoke in fluent English, he was courteous and his manners were impeccable. I pointed out the house occupied by the soldiers. He asked me why I had not left the country. I told him I was waiting for my husband to return from Yugoslavia to help me pack our belongings and settle our affairs. The colonel nodded as though he believed me, and immediately ordered one of his men to help me with the formalities required to ship my belongings out of Kuwait. I thanked him and he said: 'Now go and sleep, and don't worry.' I went back upstairs and when I looked out of the window, I saw his men enter the villa and shortly afterwards come out of it. They drove back to my building and sounded their horn. I went downstairs again and the colonel assured me I was quite safe. 'These are our élite troops,' he said. 'There is no cause for concern.' The soldiers were the Republican Guards. The next morning, I discovered a new checkpoint had been set up, less than 100 metres from my building. But, within a week, the Republican Guards had gone and the checkpoint was removed. None of the houses around had been robbed while they were there.

The day after I met the colonel I received a phone call from him. 'Is everything all right?' he asked. I told him it was and thanked him, but I wondered why he had called. A second call came a week later at 1 a.m. He asked whether my husband had returned. When I told him he hadn't, he said: 'I am going to Baghdad for a week's leave. Is there anything I can do for you there?' I politely declined. The call was brief and his manner was business-like, but I began to wonder if the colonel was going beyond the call of duty. I decided that if he phoned again, I would have to move house. As it turned out that was the last conversation I had with him.

I felt I might be robbed again in December. I had already hidden my passport, jewellery, computer and video camera in the space above the ceiling. Every time I went out I would climb on a wash-basin in the hall leading to the bathroom and hide my short-wave radio and my notes in the loft. I was planning to move at the time, but did not know where, and had arranged for most of my belongings to be stored in the basement of a house occupied by my Yugoslav friends. It took days to shift my possessions and, meanwhile, the soldiers were all around. I saw them carrying bricks, pushing wheelbarrows full of sand, while building gun-emplacements in preparation for a street war. They would stop work and look at me when I left the building. They were curious and some-times I felt they were looking up to me with some respect rather than hostility. Perhaps they thought that, under normal circumstances, we would never have been neigh-bours. They also knew I was a woman living alone and without obvious protection. I decided to speak to their officer. I found him in an unfinished villa two blocks away and appealed to his sense of decency, asking him to ensure his men behaved correctly towards me. He assured me I would have no problem from them. And I didn't. But when a new group of soldiers arrived to replace them, I was back to where I started.

One night in the third week of December I woke to the sound of breaking glass. For a moment I thought someone was trying to get into my building. I lay rigid and listened but then got up and tiptoed to the bedroom window, moving the curtain just enough to peer out. In the dark corner of our back yard there were at least four men in uniform. They were speaking in low voices. I watched them jump back and forth over the wall, taking stuff from our neighbours next door through my back yard on to the next street. They were packing their loot in plastic bags. I was terrified and did not go to sleep again until they had gone. They came again the next night and the night after, until they had systematically emptied the entire three-storey house. One night I crept on to a kitchen balcony and shouted: 'Hello, hello, who is it?' They stopped talking for a while, but then carried on. The next night I turned up the volume of my bedroom TV, but that didn't scare them away either.

By this time the United Nations had passed its resolution sanctioning the use of force against Iraq. With war looking inevitable, theft and lawlessness in Kuwait escalated. I was reluctant to go out because each time I returned home, I expected to find I had been robbed. When it did not happen, I began to believe that I had managed to avoid their attention.

After storing much of my stuff, I was finally left with four suitcases which I was going to take with me when I moved. They contained the things I needed most and liked best including some of my clothes, jewellery and books. On Christmas Eve, after going to Aziz's for a drink, I went on to a party at Danuta's. When I returned home at midnight the front door to the building was as I had left it, but inside I realised I had had, and might still have, visitors. The door to the flat downstairs was wide open and I decided not to investigate. I ran up the stairs, which were strewn with my clothes. My front door was open and there was the most horrendous mess everywhere. I jumped on to the basin and looked into the loft – my computer, jewellery and diaries were still there. Behind the Chinese screen in the living room, my Samsonite suitcase containing my best clothes was also there. They had taken a suitcase with my clothes but had left my tennis racket and the 3,000 Iraqi dinar ($1080) I stuffed inside its cover. Some Kuwaiti money I had left in the bedroom was still there. Two TV sets, a video recorder and hi-fi system had gone. Under the bed I found Basil my cat, but he was too scared to come out. I left the flat that night and never lived in it again.

XXVI

Imagine moving house on Christmas Day. I had no choice. At midnight on Christmas Eve, my flat ransacked and afraid the thieves might return, I had to find somewhere else. Vladimir Dimitrijevic was the obvious choice. He lived only half a kilometre away, he was Yugoslav and when I rushed to his house for help he immediately invited me to stay. I had been put in touch with Vladimir by Eoin two months before. He thought that I might want to have contact with someone from my homeland and on the phone Vladimir invited me to a barbecue at his flat. He had been in Kuwait for almost twenty years and he was in business as a designer and manufacturer of household items. At the time of the invasion, his wife and daughter were in Cyprus. He stayed on for fear of losing everything he had invested in his business over the years, and he was determined to see the crisis through rather than face losing the lot. He was in his mid-fifties, a warm-hearted man with a neatly trimmed beard and an impish sense of humour.

After the hostages left he offered to let me store many of my belongings in his basement. He had also equipped the basement as a shelter in case of war. A Dutch friend, Adrian Kes, lived in a flat across from him. Another flat was occupied by some Palestinians upstairs and underneath lived Mushtaq, an Iraqi who had been in Kuwait for many years. There were thousands of Iraqis living in Kuwait at the time of the invasion, which made them the subject of mutual mistrust by the Kuwaitis and the invading Iraqis. Many of them were refugees from Saddam's regime and were rounded up in the first days of the occupation. Some like Mushtaq had long been trying to emigrate to the United States. The Kuwaitis feared that they were ripe for use as informers by Saddam's troops. Some may have been if it meant saving their own skins, but most were fully integrated into Kuwaiti life and regarded Kuwait as their home and where their first loyalties lay. When they had the choice of returning to Baghdad or staying put, they chose to stay where they were.

Vladimir's flat was spacious and comfortable and reflected not only his cultivated tastes but his affinity with the Middle East. There were Turkish and Persian rugs on the floor and paintings and statuettes of Arab horses as well as attractive lampstands and coffee tables which he had designed himself. He was an accomplished horseman and had owned a pair of Arabian horses, but the Iraqis confiscated them. He was more angry about that than the looting of his factory. It had been stripped of everything, including the machinery, and shipped to Baghdad.

I was not his only guest. There was Milan, a Yugoslav architect, who had left his apartment in Sharq near the International Hotel because of a huge Iraqi military presence there. He was about forty-five and obsessed with cleanliness. He always seemed to be washing the dishes, cleaning the cooker, wiping the table. The kitchen never looked less than spotless but somehow he always managed to find something new to clean there. He was apologetic and when we ribbed him about it he laughed as much as any of us. I did less than my share of the chores, although I did do some odd jobs. Vladimir was the cook, Milan cleaned up and I took out the rubbish, when they allowed me to. It was an advantage living in a traditional

Yugoslav household where men pamper their women-folk and feel protective towards them in such crises. I indulged myself but I think they enjoyed my company. The three of us got along exceptionally well and life was cosy, and when I brought along Basil the family was complete.

A frequent visitor was Walid, a big awkward Kuwaiti who worked with Milan at the Kuwait Defence Ministry. They were close friends and while I was there they went together to Nasriya in southern Iraq to buy a flock of sheep, partly to keep busy and partly because Walid was a farmer at heart; he loved the idea of having his own farm animals. He was also a practical man and thought they would be a good investment and would in any case help with food supplies. They bought fifty lambs and carried them by truck. He had to bribe his way through army checkpoints and this cost them quite a few lambs. Their arrival caused us some amusement. He first took them to his own home on the west of the city but there was not enough room so he carried them another 15 kilometres to an empty yard next to a block of flats, owned by his father, near us in Salwa. Together, Milan and Walid built a shed for the three calves they had also bought. They spent much of their time cutting down grass and bushes in gardens close by to keep the animals fed. Then Walid bought a cow which he was told was in calf. He asked our opinion because he was afraid he may have been cheated. We all gathered around and inspected the animal. We remarked on its big stomach but I argued that all cows had big stomachs. My ignorance of such matters was exposed soon after the air war started when, to Walid's delight, the cow gave birth.

I was fond of Walid. He had studied in the United States but had none of the pretensions of other Kuwaitis who had been similarly educated. I remember him best with sleeves rolled up, working in the garden or feeding his animals, a permanent stubble on his chin and sweat on his forehead. He was a bit shy of me and felt I would be more at home among women. Every time the Iraqis made their presence felt he would express concern for my safety until finally he suggested I would be better off moving to Nuzha with his family. He came from a huge family who occupied three houses. Apart from his wife and baby there were about thirty other women and only eight men. These were his brothers and sisters, aunts and cousins. Some more men in the family had been detained and others were in hiding elsewhere.

Walid was particularly concerned about the safety of Kuwaiti women because the Iraqis were as cruel to them as they were to the resistance fighters. The evidence was apparent. In late January, Israr Al Qabandi, a woman in her mid-thirties from a prominent Kuwaiti family and herself well-educated, was killed by the Iraqis. In the first two months of the invasion she was raped by marauding troops and, in revenge, she joined the resistance and became one of its most active members, taking on some of the most dangerous missions. She is believed to have been a crucial link in maintaining communications between Kuwait and Saudi Arabia, carrying messages across the Saudi border and bringing back instructions and money to the resistance movement. She was found dead with her head split open and three bullet holes in her chest. Her name lives on as one of the heroines of the occupation. Many other women suffered almost as much. They were suspected by the Iraqis of sheltering and helping members of the resistance movement and they often distributed money to families and foreigners in hiding. In Iraqi raids on private homes, the Iraqis often took as many women as men into detention, and their humiliation was just as great. In December a group of women prisoners were stripped naked by their Iraqi jailers and forced to parade in front of the leering Iraqis. When their menfolk came to bring food and discovered what had happened, they protested. The Iraqis told them to keep quiet about it and nothing worse would happen to the women.

When Walid advised me to move in with his women-folk, I politely declined, mainly because I had settled in and was happy with life in the flat. I was glad I stayed where I was because Walid's fears for the women turned out to be justified. Soon after the air war began, one of his female cousins and her mother were arrested. The mother was later released but his cousin was hanged by a chain in a detention centre. Walid and his relatives found her body left on a rubbish tip a few days before the Iraqi withdrawal. Another cousin, an army officer, who abandoned his uni-form when the Iraqis invaded and got a job with a local dairy, was arrested for holding Kuwaiti currency which had been outlawed. By liberation day, Walid still did not know whether he was dead or alive.

The break-in at my flat had wrecked my Christmas Day. I was to have spent it with Rose Lambert and her Kuwaiti boyfriend. Instead, I returned to my flat to try to salvage what was left of my belongings. I was determined not to miss the next party. It was held at the home of Lorraine Dyer, like Rose a British girl with a Kuwaiti boyfriend. Apart from a few expatriates like myself, most Western women had stayed on because their husbands or boy-friends were Kuwaitis and in Lorraine's case because she had lived in Kuwait all her life. Some of these girls were under extreme pressure from their parents to return home. And there were many distressing messages coming over the Gulf Link begging them to come back. Some did and then found themselves worried about the fate of their menfolk. Some of those who stayed were equally anguished about their parents' concern. But there was a solid core of about ten who were convinced that they were right to stay and for whom Kuwait was their first home.

Like me, these women did all they could to maintain contact with their parents and relatives in Britain and had as much difficulty as I did. The satellite phones were in huge demand, but their scarcity value and the need for secrecy made them accessible only to a few of us with Kuwaiti insiders. It was Hani who presented me with my best Christmas and New Year's present, a telephone call. Adrian and I were in the first group to use the satellite phone, and on December 28 Hani took us on a circuitous route with a number of stops before finally arriving at a house in Sabah Al Salem, a sprawling new neighbourhood south of Salwa. There were two other Britons, Geoffrey French, a businessman, and Heather Rennison the wife of a Kuwaiti. The satellite dish was on the roof but the phone was in a small room. There were about twelve of us altogether inside and the Kuwaiti was operating the equipment. Everyone was excited, including the geese outside, which were making a terrible racket. Heather spoke first telling her parents she was safe and not to worry. We all listened in and later she told us what her parents had said. Privacy was irrelevant throughout the occupation – we were too close not to share each other's joys as well as hardships. I spoke to my sister in Turin, who was overjoyed to hear my voice. It was the first time I had spoken to any of my family since July and I was anxious to know how they were, but also whether they were angry about my staying on. I was relieved when she said that they were not, though they were worried. At that point she broke down, but I managed to reassure her and the conversation ended on a happy note. For others, it was not such a happy occasion. Adrian learnt his mother had died, and I learnt that Sandy was attending his father's funeral from his wife Barbara. Subsequent groups were in for a disappointment; they never made their calls because the security situation suddenly worsened and the Kuwaitis were afraid they might be discovered.

On New Year's Eve we all got a cake from the Kuwaitis as well as 1,000 Iraqi dinar ($90). The British ambassador left behind greeting cards and a bottle of Scotch each. We drank to his health. There was no shortage of New Year's Eve parties, although some people declined invitations because they were too afraid of thieves to leave their homes unattended. Vladimir and Adrian didn't want to take the risk and stayed at home. I wanted to use the opportunity to say goodbye to some of my friends. After failing to get our residence papers, Lise and I were due to leave by January 13. Neither of us took it seriously and if we were going anywhere it would be into hiding. But we did not know how strictly the Iraqis would apply the rules and whether there would be a new hunt for foreigners as the January 15 deadline of the United Nation's ultimatum expired. With war set to begin, this could be our last New Year celebration. I was determined to let my hair down. My first port of call was Lorraine's. She was about thirty and lived close by, and the party had barely begun when I arrived. Inside, there was nothing to suggest that anything untoward was going on outside. People were chatting happily and everyone was dressed up to the nines. Lorraine looked wonderful with her hair up, and was wearing some of her most striking jewellery. Lise looked even more startling in an electric-blue silk ball gown. I was distinctly underdressed in my sweater and corduroys. There was plenty of food and drink and the guests were mainly Britons, Danes and Kuwaitis. I left before it was in full swing because I wanted to be at Elisabeth Nowacka's flat by midnight, a ten-minute drive away, roadblocks permitting. I was not stopped, and arrived to discover a note on the door, just like old times, saying the party was on the sixth floor. Such signs were common before the invasion, when people found it difficult to locate parties in new neighbourhoods. Inside there was a motley crowd of Indians, Kuwaitis and Poles, as well as Elisabeth's Danish husband and two Iraqi doctors who had been living in Kuwait for a long while. Again, there was plenty of food and drink as well as fire crackers, funny hats and face masks, and when midnight came the room erupted with the noise of plastic trumpets, taped music and loud shouts and squeals. We all cried and hugged each other. I danced non-stop for two hours and left at two o'clock, looking dishevelled and with iridescent sticks in my hair. I stopped at several checkpoints, loudly wished soldiers a Happy New Year and, though puzzled, they waved me through, murmuring their own greetings.

Our celebrations were shortlived. In the second week of January a car pulled up outside Vladimir's flat and two men in plain clothes stepped out. Vladimir went out to speak to them. They refused to say who they were but their new car had no number plates. They asked Vladimir how many people lived in the building and what their nationalities were. Then they went to Adrian's flat and to the building next door. We were sure they were members of Mukhabarat.

Salwa was teeming with troops, particularly our street which linked the Fahaheel expressway with the coast road. In early January they moved into two schools and began fortifying them as if expecting an attack. We were about 100 metres from the beach where the Iraqis had already built foxholes and dug in with tanks and artillery.

We felt even more hemmed in by soldiers, and the arrival of the secret police made things worse. Over the next few days we had three more visits from different people and in different cars but asking the same questions. The Iraqis had begun a new wave of arresting foreigners without residence permits, including hundreds of Indians and Filipinos, who were detained at market places and road-blocks. The word was that they would be deported and taken to Basra.

On Friday January 11, despite fears that I might be caught, I went ahead with my usual trip to Aziz's place in Shuwaikh. They were all seated around the swimming pool as usual, although one Pakistani architect was missing. He had been one of those picked up and taken to Basra. A French woman had also been detained and Aziz's niece Najat advised me to move to Shuwaikh for my own safety. On my return home, Milan told me he had been questioned by an Iraqi we thought was from the secret police. He had examined his passport and said he would return in the morning when we were all at home. It was the nudge I needed to leave. It was another sad parting because I felt thoroughly at home in Vladimir's flat. But I hardened my heart and packed for the umpteenth time. It was January 12, the day before my own deadline ran out to leave the country and three days before the UN deadline expired for Iraq to pull out or else. Soon after I left, an Iraqi general moved into the flat next door to Vladimir's.

XXVII

The advantages of moving to Shuwaikh outweighed the dangers, I reasoned. Salwa had been home to so many Westerners that, if the Iraqis were going to round up more, this is where they would start. But Westerners were few and far between in Shuwaikh and the last place the Iraqis would look for them. They had also completed most of their sweeps of the area for dissident Kuwaitis and those remaining were now relatively safe. There was always the risk that the Iraqis might return and that risk was enhanced if a Westerner was found in their midst. The penalty for harbouring a Westerner who had been ordered to leave the country might not mean the blowing up of a house, as had formerly been the case, but it might still mean detention.

Shuwaikh covers a wide area, including the port and the university campus as well as the industrial sector with hundreds of workshops and newspaper offices. The residential area was small but exclusive and most of its residents were wealthy Kuwaitis. Aziz Sultan was one of them. Several members of his family had homes in the area, including Najat's brothers who lived next door to each other but were out of the country. I had understood from Najat that I could move into one, sharing with Karl Okart, an American architect. The other one was occupied by Jim Rankin, a Scotsman, and his family. When I arrived, it seemed I had misunderstood. Karl wasn't at home and Najat was reluctant to let me stay without his permission. I was about to return to Salwa and face whatever was in store for me there when Aziz came to the rescue and suggested I move in with him.

It was a lovely house and beautifully furnished. Aziz spent only his days there and his nights with his brothers in Mishref, 25 kilometres away. His Goanese maid Florenta was also there and so was the Egyptian watchman. The surroundings were peaceful and there was not a soldier in sight. A high wall surrounded the villa and the only ones I ever saw were those manning the gun emplacements on the rooftops of the Sheraton Hotel about 200 metres away. Aziz had a satellite dish on the roof where we could pick up the American Cable News Network television service. There was plenty of food and I did not want for comfort.

At first I missed the company of Vladimir and his friends; here I was isolated and alone for much of the time. Aziz and his wife and children looked down from the photographs on the shelves. They were in the United States. At first I felt like an intruder and Aziz was polite, but reserved. He was not a typical Kuwaiti, and didn't look like one. A tall, greying man of fifty with fair complexion and light brown eyes, he was as distinguished-looking as befitted the head of the Gulf Bank. I had met him along with his friends on many occasions during my Friday visits and, although friendly, he was always slightly distant and private. He rarely talked about himself and he did not like socialising. One of his relatives told me: 'You cannot invite Aziz to a party. He goes to bed at 9 o'clock so that he can get up at 4 a.m. to go jogging.' I saw something of his disciplined routine. He exercised daily in his gym inside the house which was fitted out with all kinds of equipment. He also went jogging and even played basketball in a nearby school. He used every moment of his time. He was devoted to his wife and family and wrote to them regularly. I think he was also writing about the occupation. He read a good deal, did some gardening and his only relaxation was the odd spot of sunbathing.

I grew to learn that he was deeply involved in political opposition in Kuwait and much of his time was spent, I suspect, in meetings with other opposition members. He talked to me on occasion about his political views and said he was unhappy about the situation before the invasion. He wanted to see political institutions based on Western democratic models introduced and foresaw the need for a wholesale shake-up if the country were to become a united force. He feared that violence would come in the wake of the liberation between opposing factions of royalists and democrats and he felt that the mass of the people might be driven to rebel against their old rulers.

By the time I arrived in Shuwaikh the Geneva talks between the US Secretary of State, James Baker, and the Iraqi Foreign Minister, Tareq Aziz, had ended in failure, and when the UN Secretary General Perez de Cuellar's last-minute mission to Baghdad also failed, we knew it was only a question of time before war began. The Iraqis were already pulling out their civil administration and had told those with ration cards to use them before January 10. Of the ration cards issued 100,000 went to Palestinians and eleven to Kuwaiti families – a sign of Palestinian compliance with the laws of the Iraqis and the rejection of them by Kuwaitis.

Foreigners, mostly Asians, were being picked up for deportation and the curfew which had been lifted in November was to be reimposed on January 14. The Iraqis were also planning to stop civilian air and road traffic in and out of Kuwait. Their troops had taken up fortified positions in trenches and bunkers along the seafront and had placed 'Doshka' – multi-purpose air and ground guns

– on flyovers and high buildings overlooking intersections and roundabouts. A metal barrier had been
planted along coastal waters to ward against an amphibious landing. Rumours persisted that the Iraqis were withdrawing, but there was no evidence to support them. On
the contrary, Iraq looked as though it was gearing up for
war.

As far as Aziz was concerned, Iraq's was a ragtag army
that would be defeated in double quick time by any allied
offensive. He ruled out any bombing or street fighting in
residential areas and he thought we would all survive.
We nevertheless wasted no time in making our preparations for war, just in case he was wrong. President
Bush had said it would be sooner rather than later and
we sensed we were living in the last days of the occupation. The glass on the sliding doors dividing the swimming
pool from the sitting room was already taped against
bomb blasts. We had soon taped the rest of the windows
and were planning a shelter for Florenta, the watchman
and me in the pump room. We thought the war would
begin at night while Aziz would be at Mishref.

Many Kuwaiti villas and apartment blocks had basements and, all over the city, people were converting them
into shelters. As usual some owners couldn't resist
outdoing their neighbours. One friend told me: 'I've just
seen a basement which looked more like Disneyland.'
While some families were only concerned with the safety
of their own, others opened up their basements for general use and posted notices outside, inviting the public to
use them.

Our pump room was below ground level. Aziz produced some rugs and with blankets and pillows, we made
it quite comfortable. He moved in a radiator to make it
dry and warm and Florenta and I brought canned food
and bottled water. We also made a list of what else we

211

would need if the time came, including towels, a radio, a torch, a can-opener and a kettle. In case the water should be cut off, Aziz filled the swimming pool, and I parked my car in the car port out of harm's way. The watchman bolted the gate with the iron bars, which was just as well. On the evening of January 15 a group of soldiers came to the house next door where Jim's jeep was parked outside. Three of them were armed and Jim had little choice but to watch them drive away in it.

That night, I sat watching CNN news while I wrote up my despatch on the way Kuwaitis were preparing for war. At 2.40 a.m. CNN interrupted its programme to go over to its reporters in Baghdad. The Iraqi capital was under allied air attack. The three correspondents were describing in turns what they were watching. I was equally wide-eyed. The Baghdad sky was alight with anti-aircraft tracer fire and I could hear the rumbling of the jet planes and the crunch of explosions. But that was just on TV. I had heard no sound of aircraft passing over on their way. The war had begun and, like the invasion, we first heard about it from an overseas broadcast.

XXVIII

I had waited for almost six months for this moment. I had never had any doubt that Kuwait would be free again, the only question was when. Now my second, more secret wish was about to be fulfilled. I would experience war. This was going to be my war and, overcome with the exhilaration of fear, I did not think of what the costs might be. I was longing to share this moment with someone and I began calling friends, one by one, to tell them the news. Everyone seemed relieved that the long wait was over. We all were aware of the dangers and that we could get caught in the crossfire, but if this were to happen so be it. We had chosen to stay knowing the risks.

There was nothing else to do. I stretched on the sofa, lit a cigarette and watched the bombing of Baghdad. I felt safe and comfortable. Baghdad was far away.

Just before 4 a.m. I went down to the kitchen to make a cup of coffee. The silence was deadly. Then suddenly there was a tremendous blast, first one, then another and a third. It sounded like the biggest battle ever was raging in our garden. I felt sick. The pump room, I thought, I must get to the pump room. I rushed to a door which led outside. It was locked and there was no key in it. I turned to another which led to the back garden. It too was locked and there was no key. I panicked. The house will collapse on me and I can't get out, I thought.

'Florenta-a-a,' I screamed.

Just as I started for the living room she came in from the car-port side carrying her bag and jacket. She was giggling. She always did that, whether the news was good or bad. We ran through the living room and out. The pump room seemed miles away and I thought we would never make it. The noise was deafening and we ran down the ladder. Once below the ground, I remembered I had left all the things I planned to take with me in the house. Florenta at least had had the presence of mind to bring her bag and towel with her. This was our only defence against chemical attack. Then the watchman appeared with a box of food we had prepared. Now the three of us just stood and listened. It was impossible to tell whether the explosions were bombs or anti-aircraft guns firing at the aircraft flying overhead on their way to Baghdad.

In less than ten minutes we were back in the house. The guns had fallen silent, dawn was breaking and the only sounds were those of neighbours calling out to each other to make sure they were safe.

We began to move all we had planned to take into the pump room. Now that the war had started we knew there would be more explosions and the next time they might be closer. The next attack came just before 9 a.m. and we were ready for it. It lasted for almost twenty minutes and, down in the pump room, I began to distinguish the sounds. There was a rumble of what must have been fighter planes or bombers. Then gunfire started from the batteries set up in positions close to our home. They were the noisiest, especially when combined with the deafening sound of the automatic weapons.

There were still no bombs falling on Shuwaikh, though later in the day we did hear the sound of distant bombing, a kind of thumping noise that rattled our glass doors. I saw the canvas on the painting quiver and sometimes the vibrations shook the whole house. By this time we were upstairs again and we never went back to the pump room throughout the war. We became used to the noise, even when it grew closer when outlying districts of the city were bombed. All the while the Iraqis kept up their anti-aircraft fire.

From then on I began to sleep on the sofa in the TV room anxious not to miss any news on CNN. On the second day of the air war, Friday January 18, I was awakened just before 5 a.m. by an excited voice on the TV. There had been a Scud missile attack on Israel and there were fears that the rockets carried chemical warheads. I was suddenly wide awake. I recalled that Saddam had threatened to turn Kuwait into a graveyard if the allies attacked. I also remembered the words of an Iraqi officer as they were recounted to me by a Palestinian friend: 'If the invasion was bad, the withdrawal, forced or voluntary, would be worse.' Now as I listened to the sirens wailing in Tel Aviv and saw the Israelis in their shelters with their gas masks on, I realised we were in danger of exposure to a similar attack.

Although Saddam never used his chemical weapons and the Scuds did relatively little damage in Israel and Saudi Arabia, both countries were better prepared than we were for these attacks. We had no early warning systems, no gas masks and no Patriots. All Florenta, the watchman, and I had was masking tape to seal the doors and windows. Vladimir and Adrian did likewise while Zeinab and her family cut up plastic rubbish bags and turned them into protective suits. Some Kuwaitis were even more ingenious. They kept their chickens close by in the belief that they would serve as an early warning to a poisonous gas attack. We began watching the sparrows in our gardens hoping they would never stop chirping. At one point there was a rumour that gas masks were available at KD 50 ($180) each. The Iraqi soldiers had them and we believed this was the source. I signed up

215

for ten masks for me and my friends, but we never got any. Some people had smog masks while others got the type used by doctors in hospitals.

My Egyptian friend Nabeel urged me to make my own. He gave me the recipe: 'Crush some charcoal and toast it for about ten minutes,' he said. 'Then stuff it into a sock, distributing it evenly, and tie it over your nose and mouth.' It sounded very inefficient so I never bothered. I thought my best bet was the swimming pool. I would jump in with a towel and stay under water until forced to surface. Then, with a towel over my head, I would grab a breath of air before diving again. Then I realised the water would get contaminated, so I scrapped the idea.

The destruction caused by the Scuds showed how useless the sealing of windows and doors was and, anyway, the pump room was impossible to seal. I debated for days where to run first if an attack came. The biggest question was how would we know if we were being gassed? David Dunn, the American pastor, had given me his poison-gas treatment kit before leaving. I now read and re-read the instructions, but was none the wiser. David had also given me tablets to counter an attack by biological weapons. The instructions on the bottle recommended one half of a tablet every eight hours but starting when, it didn't say. I decided to leave the entire problem to fate.

These thoughts were largely driven away by glowing reports of allied successes. In the first news conference, the American Secretary of Defence, Dick Cheney, and the head of the Joint Chiefs of Staff, General Colin Powell, could hardly contain their excitement, as they reeled off the list of successes against Iraqi airbases, missile sites and installations, including the destruction of Iraq's nuclear reactors. Some got carried away, including a CNN reporter who claimed the Republican Guard had been decimated. He also commented: 'This could be a very short war.'

In the five weeks that followed life took on a surreal quality. I was in hiding, yet I lived in a beautiful villa. Sometimes I felt like a bird in a golden cage. We could hear the war but we could not see it. The war was all about Kuwait and its freedom, yet if Kuwait were mentioned, it was only in passing. The relentless bombing of Iraq and its forces took priority. There was nothing about us, no message. When American generals in Saudi Arabia were occasionally asked what their advice was to those in Kuwait they would say: 'Keep faith.'

We were at the heart of the conflict, yet the flames and destruction never reached us. Hardly a night went by without gunfire. At the sound of the aircraft approaching, the Iraqi gunners would go berserk and bang away. I would lie in bed and listen. There was first a distant rumble of an allied plane and, within seconds, the Iraqis would start up. The sliding glass doors would rattle and the whole house shake. Then the machine-guns would crackle and all Iraq's orchestral arsenal would rise to a crescendo. Sometimes a muezzin (prayer leader) in the nearby mosque would compete by calling the faithful to morning prayer, his voice audible only in the brief pauses between gunfire and explosions. Then silence would follow, broken only by the wail of a neighbourhood cat or a crying child.

There was criticism from some Western television audiences when a CNN correspondent described the air battles over Baghdad as being like a fireworks display; the objection was that it sounded as though he was describing a carnival and not a war. But the description was accurate nevertheless. There were nights when I ran into the garden at the sound of gunfire to watch the skies erupt in a dazzling explosion of green, red and white stars. At the sound of approaching planes, people would rush outside and cheer like football fans, and others would shout: 'Smash them.' We would strain to catch a glimpse of the aircraft, which flew high and were only dots in the sky during the day and invisible at night. Mostly we would see the small puffs of smoke from exploding Iraqi groundfire.

Although bombing raids were taking place in Kuwait it was impossible for me to judge their distance. The Kuwaiti airbases well away from the city which had been captured by the Iraqis were being bombed as was Bubiyan Island, one of the two seized on the first day of the invasion. The raids got closer and windows were shattered at homes in Mishref and Salwa during one allied air attack on Iraqi positions at what had been the headquarters of Kuwait's Sixth Armoured Brigade. This was just off the Sixth Ring Road some 30 kilometres away from the city. Another raid close by destroyed an ammunition dump in Sabhan and my friends told me of seeing the flames leaping high in the sky and hearing repeated explosions as the arsenal went up.

In the early hours of one morning I heard the biggest bang so far. At the time I didn't know where it came from but later that day an American general told a televised briefing in Saudi Arabia that helicopters had destroyed several Iraqi patrol boats in Kuwait Bay, in which Shuwaikh Port was located. That would have been only about a kilometre away from our villa. I was tempted at the time to go on to the roof to see what had happened but in the light of Hani's experience didn't dare. A few days before Hani had gone on his roof to watch the 'fireworks' and immediately found himself under fire from Iraqi troops, apparently afraid of having their positions revealed by signalling. He made a quick descent, as did many other Kuwaitis trying to get a closer glimpse of the air war over Kuwait.

When once I made a daytime visit to the roof I found I was in full view of Iraqi gun emplacements positioned on the rooftops of nearby villas which they had taken over during the course of their occupation. I never went up again although we occasionally scanned the city from Jim's roof which was not that exposed.

At one point missiles were thought to have landed in two densely populated suburbs of the city at Yarmouk and Mishref. They landed on wasteground, causing little damage. Aziz described a piece of metal, more than a metre long but which might, he thought, have been an empty fuel tank jettisoned by an aircraft rather than a missile. There was another report that a missile had hit a shopping centre in the city. There was never any official confirmation of this but I later saw damage at the centre which could have been caused by a bomb, a missile or shellfire. The raids went on day and night and we sometimes saw fires raging in the distance and columns of smoke rising south of us towards the desert. But most of the time we heard more of the war than we saw and despite our close proximity to it, learned of its progress mainly from TV and radio like the rest of the world.

One manifestation of the conflict came with the arrival of black rain at the end of January, soon after the Iraqis began setting fire to the oil wells. At first it appeared in little black puddles after a shower. Then Haya Al Mughni called one day and said they could no longer eat vegetables from their garden. They washed them over and over again but the vegetables remained black. By the middle of February dense dark clouds gathered over the horizon, blocking the sun and sending us into a semi-permanent twilight. When it rained, black specks fell with it and stood out on the white garden furniture and the turquoise water of the pool. This was the rainy season and one of the wettest in thirty years. The clouds, mixed with the smoke from the burning oil fields, combined to press down on the city, lowering the temperature and blackening our spirits. It had the characteristics of a nuclear winter.

I hardly went out; most people didn't, including the Kuwaitis. The Iraqis were not only manning their artillery and infantry defences, they were still carrying out neighbourhood patrols around the city. I never saw any because we bolted and barred our high gates. We also took the precaution of unscrewing panels in bedroom wardrobes in which to hide my British passport, diary and press cuttings.

The Iraqis were now confiscating cars as a matter of course in preparation for their withdrawal. They were stepping up their searches, detaining and often killing those suspected of links with the resistance with a new ruthlessness, knowing that they were soon to leave. The Iraqi crackdown followed an upsurge in the activities of the resistance movement, which had launched several attacks immediately the air war broke out. They began attacking checkpoints and sentry posts.

Jerzy, my Polish friend, described how his Kuwaiti neighbour became irritated by an anti-aircraft gun near his home. One night, armed with a rifle, the Kuwaiti climbed on to his roof, took careful aim and shot the anti-aircraft gunner from his position on top of a water tower. Neighbours spoke of hearing a thump as he hit the ground. The next day the Iraqis moved the gun and conducted a house-to-house search of the area. They never found the marksman.

Aziz was one who refused to allow his activities to be curtailed. He continued to run the gauntlet of army patrols and checkpoints in his daily shuttle between

Shuwaikh and Mishref. We were on formal but friendly terms. He made it clear he did not want me to have visitors for security reasons and he was not too happy about my frequent use of the phone. I protested that I could not live in isolation but I understood his point of view. He also did not like my smoking, having himself given up some five years before. He was so tactful that it took him ages to state his objections and then he admitted he had achieved it only after some days of wrestling with the problem.

As a liberal-minded person, he felt that democracy began at home. I was glad that he spoke out. He was an extremely kind and considerate person and I was aware that he was providing me with a safe place; it was just that I was tense during the many hours I spent alone, and cigarettes and the phone were my main relief.

We did not allow the war and the searches to interrupt our occasional get-togethers. Indeed, we needed them more than ever. The threat from inside now extended to one from outside and threw us more closely together. We felt there was safety in numbers and it enabled us to talk away our fears and helped us forget the worst that might happen. Najat and Karl were regular visitors. Jim also sometimes came and so did some of Aziz's Kuwaiti friends. The heart and soul of some of these get-togethers was Leila Al Qadi, an English lecturer at Kuwait University. Leila had a lively mind and astute political brain. She aroused some disapproval from fellow-Kuwaitis, and cut across most of their conventions: drinking, smoking and airing her views on the world at large, including men. She was married to an Algerian businessman and had two children and she made it four when she fostered two waifs from an orphanage which was taken over by the Iraqis and used to billet troops. When more traditional

221

Kuwaitis heard of the adoptions she was immediately welcomed back into the fold.

On these occasions Aziz came more out of his shell; he was more comfortable in company. He was a Kuwaiti of strong principles who kept a remarkably cool head throughout the crisis. He was also an influential political figure behind the scenes in the opposition movement. And while he expressed his views candidly, he did not waste words and preferred to listen. I felt a better person for knowing him. Aziz predicted that the war would be over by February 15. Impossible, I said. The Iraqis were still entrenched in the city and the suburbs and, despite the relentless allied air raids, Baghdad was giving no sign of backing down. The ground war, once it began, would drag on for at least a month or two, I argued.

February 15 was a Friday, the war was still going on but, unbeknown to us, the day marked the beginning of the end of the Iraqi occupation. On that day Baghdad announced it was willing to withdraw from Kuwait.

XXIX

The Iraqi announcement was made while I was having lunch at Leila's. There were about ten of us and we were so scornful of any promises coming from Baghdad that we refused to interrupt lunch to watch CNN news. We felt justified when we later discovered what the proposals were. There were strings attached and Washington dismissed the plan outright. The war continued. But if *we* weren't rejoicing, the Iraqi troops were on a high. Hours after the announcement, they were firing their guns into the air in premature celebration. In the process they wounded some twenty Kuwaitis. Their delight at the prospect of pulling out confirmed what we had always suspected: they did not want to fight and their morale was low.

We saw the allied victory as a foregone conclusion: it was only a question of whether it would come this month or the next. But things had begun moving fast in the world outside and we did not always understand what was going on. Much of it revolved around a Soviet peace package, though the details were by no means clear. The Iraqis talked to the Soviets, the Soviets talked to the Americans and the French went their own way.

On Friday, February 22, President Bush gave the Iraqis an ultimatum: twenty-four hours to get out of Kuwait. His decision came as something of a surprise for us. It removed any doubts we might have had that the air war would drag on leaving us holed up and fearful for months. We saw it as the ultimate expression of the allies' sense of supremacy and could not help feeling the end of our hide-and-seek game with the Iraqis was in sight.

In the afternoon, Aziz's brother Khalid came to pick him up for a trip to Mishref. He also brought us fresh vegetables from his garden; he had been our only source since the war began. Before leaving, Aziz told me the Iraqis had again stepped up their street patrols and that if they were unable to avoid the checkpoints, they would return to Shuwaikh. Later that afternoon Jerzy came to visit me with Ahmed, a young Kuwaiti who lived two houses away. His teenage brother had just been released after a week in detention, but there were new reports of Kuwaitis being rounded up wholesale, in the streets and also in the mosques. A neighbour, Tariq, was picked up and, later, Ghanim Najar, a university lecturer and columnist on *Al Watan* newspaper who had cycled to visit us earlier in the month. From his house in the next street Karl had seen Iraqi soldiers arrest two Kuwaitis. Later we discovered many more than we thought had been detained or had disappeared.

Throughout the afternoon we listened to the repeated roar of Iraqi artillery guns. The land war had not begun and we could not figure out what they were shooting at.

On Saturday Aziz failed to come home, for the first time since the air war had begun. By that time the phones had been out for more than two weeks and I had no way of checking if he had arrived safely in Mishref. But I did not read too much into his absence: I knew he was daring, but also careful.

Saturday was also the day of the Bush deadline. It came and went and, from what we could see and hear, the Iraqis did not budge. On the contrary, all afternoon there was a horrendous crashing noise that sounded like thunder repeatedly striking the ground. It crossed my mind they might have been blowing up buildings.

The 8 p.m. deadline passed and that night all we could see from Jim's roof was the glow of fires in the sky south of Shuwaikh. The whole city was in darkness because the Iraqis had switched off street lighting. There was no movement anywhere and the silence was deadly. Since our satellite dish had packed up, I stayed at Jim's to listen to CNN news. The Russians made some vague noises to the effect that the Iraqis had accepted the 'American statement'. Iraq apparently was still trying to salvage what it could of its face. President Bush would have none of it and gave the green light for the ground offensive.

Knowing this, I kicked myself the next morning when I got up at 10 a.m. to find that I had overslept the beginning of the ground war by a whole six hours. Throughout the occupation I had never risen so late. But I had a good excuse. On that Sunday, the day never dawned. Earlier, I had looked through the gap between the curtains and had seen that it was still dark outside. I thought it was too early to get up and went on dozing. It wasn't early. The air was grey and polluted and smelled of kerosene. It was the first day of the ground war and we were having our first experience of night-time at noon.

Karl and I sat on the doorstep of the lounge overlooking the front garden and stared in wonder at the sky. Layers of clouds and smoke travelled fast and low, turning and twisting as if moved by a hurricane. The sun looked like the moon and the air became cold. The ships offshore had stopped shelling, the skies were empty of planes and the Iraqi batteries were stilled. It was eerily silent. This was a strange war, I thought. It was not like two armies colliding, more as if some invisible hand from above had declared war on the world. We went in and lit a kerosene lamp.

When it brightened a bit later, I went into the street and saw that the Sheraton Hotel had been blackened by fire and the gun emplacements on the roof were unmanned. By then we had heard the Iraqis were destroying public buildings with tank fire and setting them ablaze. Musa'ad, my Kuwaiti neighbour, said the Meridien Hotel and the parliament building had also been hit by tank fire.

That night I again went over to Jim's. Musa'ad had lent him a generator and we saw the first television pictures of the battlefield and Iraqi soldiers surrendering. They looked pitiful and I was glad they would be treated in a humane and civilised manner. Violence breeds violence, I thought, and we were tired of brutality and destruction.

At his news conference General Schwarzkopf reported the facts sparingly, but what he said pointed to a huge allied success. A Pentagon source quoted on CNN said Kuwait might be only hours away from liberation. This was Sunday, February 24, and the next day was Kuwait's National Day. 'We may be free tomorrow,' I said to Karl. He looked unmoved. He had earlier seen some Iraqi soldiers sneaking around the neighbourhood. He was wary of any public statements, whatever their source. While we watched TV, a small flame shot up from the satellite receiver resting on the TV set. There was no damage but the receiver burnt out and that was the end of our TV viewing.

Outside, the darkness was impenetrable. I held my arms stretched out in front of me like a blind woman as I was crossing the street to our gate, afraid I might bump into somebody. I had a torch but didn't dare use it in case the Iraqis spotted me.

The next day, Monday February 25, the guns started up again and I set about organising our life to cope with fresh problems. There was now no electricity and our tanks were nearly empty of water. As we needed water to flush the toilet, we filled buckets from the pool, which was getting increasingly dirty. Florenta lit the barbecue to save cooking with gas. The logs we had cut with Aziz burnt fast, but we had a good supply. I prepared some dough for bread rolls and we baked them on the barbecue. It was not ideal, but it worked and the bread tasted good. All the while, the bombs and artillery roared in the background. Radio news was claiming the US Marines and allied Arab forces were closing in on the city. I wondered whether there would be street fighting. I had heard noises in the night which sounded like trucks and tanks on the road. But the Iraqi troops had moved frequently and I had ignored it.

On Tuesday, February 26, I woke up to the crackle of automatic weapon fire. On the radio all stations carried the latest news. Saddam Hussein had ordered a full-scale withdrawal. The gunfire continued well into the morning and I cursed the Iraqis for disobeying their orders. It was the first time that they had done so in seven months. The firing became more sporadic, and about noon, when I was in the middle of kneading dough for the bread I was making, a car pulled up in front of my gate. A familiar figure, his face unshaven and his dishdasha and gutra dishevelled, got out and I ran to greet him. It was Aziz, back again for the first time in three days.

'The Iraqis are withdrawing,' he said. I flung my hands up in delight and realised they were covered in dough.

The people of Mishref were already celebrating, Aziz said. Though he warned me that Iraqi soldiers were still roaming the streets and Shuwaikh was not yet safe. But after almost seven months in hiding, moving from one refuge to another, dodging night patrols and checkpoints, this was not the time for caution. I wanted to see for myself.

I was joined by Karl and together we made for the street and headed towards the roundabout in front of the Sheraton. We moved cautiously. I could still hear shooting not far away and I was in no mood to get killed at this late stage. We edged our way along, hugging walls, and soon ran into other little groups of Kuwaitis who, like us, were making their first tentative steps to freedom, looking over their shoulders as if half-expecting to be taken by surprise.

Freedom Day was being celebrated at the Sheraton roundabout. A dozen people soon grew to two dozen. On the way we were joined by a group of Kuwaiti women and children and when they saw us they began ululating and shouting 'Mabrouk, mabrouk,' – Congratulations. Everyone was united by relief.

I ran ahead, shaking hands with anyone in sight: neighbours I knew and people I had never seen before. It was a wonderful moment. A jeep with two young Kuwaitis, their heads wrapped in red-checked winter qutras, pulled up in the road. They were carrying rifles. They pointed them at the sky and fired into the air. A man of about forty produced a hammer and began trying to destroy the tiled portrait of Saddam Hussein which had been erected in the middle of the roundabout. It was a ridiculously inadequate tool and he could only manage to chip off the edges and disfigure the face.

I ran to an abandoned Iraqi gun emplacement and then to a jeep that had been left on the roundabout. The Iraqis left behind live ammunition, uniforms, and picture magazines. Strewn near by were a number of music cassettes. In the jeep were tins of Kraft cheese, a pair of red woman's shoes and a brand new china tea-set. There was an unopened bottle of nail polish. I stood on the roundabout and felt like shouting. I think this was when the realisation that the Iraqis had fled really sunk in.

They had left overnight – a neighbour had seen them set off about 11 p.m. in a state of wild confusion and in a convoy of stolen cars, buses and trucks as well as in tanks and armoured personnel carriers. I imagined their fear. I remembered the fear that had been with me for much of the time since August. This made it almost worthwhile.

'We've made it, we've made it!' I shouted. Then I stuffed my pockets with bullets and rejoined Karl to examine the blackened walls of the Sheraton Hotel. Inside, it had been gutted. It was there we met Talal. He invited us to join him and his friend in their Chevy. We had no idea he was on a man-hunting expedition.

After witnessing the incident with the lone Iraqi soldier in which he exchanged fire with Talal but managed to escape, we began a tour of the city. I saw for the first time the full extent of the devastation. At the municipality building two Iraqi flags were still flying and Karl and I each tore one away from its wire mooring. I threw mine on to the ground and stamped on it. Karl put his in his pocket and kept it as a souvenir. We approached a nearby house, half-afraid there might still be Iraqi soldiers inside. Inside, a dim light reflected on the glass doors and, as we went closer, we discovered it was a candle, still burning, though the Iraqis had gone.

On the road we passed masses of abandoned jeeps and tanks. At the Dasman Palace there were carloads of Kuwaitis. Many had ventured into the palace grounds for the first time in their lives, as if on a sightseeing tour of a stately home. We didn't stop long. Talal drove on to a stretch of wasteland close to the British Embassy on the seafront, where the Iraqis had built trenches and bunkers. I was afraid we might run over a mine at any moment.

It was now about two in the afternoon. The grey sky which had overhung Kuwait for almost two weeks darkened even further and the rain suddenly began to pour down. It was a welcome relief, clearing the air of the acrid smell of the oil from the wells burning away in the desert. By now we had toured much of the city. It had not only been ransacked, torn apart and blackened by fires, it had been defiled. Litter was scattered everywhere, an appalling stench was coming from the buildings the Iraqis had occupied, and messages they had sprayed on the walls said they would return to recapture Kuwait.

When Talal said he had a surprise for us, I was excited. I needed something to lift the gloom that had suddenly descended.

He drove west to the district of Kheifan where we stopped outside the house of a Kuwaiti businessman, Hilal Al Mutairi, who was out of the country. A man at the door told Karl to hand over his revolver and a woman asked for my identity card. I didn't have it with me, but Talal vouched for me. Inside, there was complete darkness, until someone brought a kerosene lamp. Under its light, I made out eight Iraqi soldiers. They had been captured the night before and they were sitting crosslegged on the floor. They looked up surprised to see Karl and me, and were immediately anxious to talk. They raised their hands like schoolboys asking for permission to speak. The one with most to say was Muslim Hussain, a former labourer from the southern Iraqi town of Kerbala, a Shi'ite stronghold. He had a wife and five children and had been seized, he said, on the street and press-ganged into the army. He was a veteran of the war with Iran, in which he had lost two brothers. What he wanted, he said, was to live peacefully with his family. He and the other seven had been captured by two Kuwaitis. Their officers had told them to make their own way home to Iraq.

They described how they had come under attack from the Kuwaitis and had been used by their officers as shields. The officers had then fled. One of them was a seventeen-year-old called Ali. He had been taken from school in Baghdad and also forced into the army. He was the quietest and sat silently in the corner of the room, his eyes almost pleading with fear.

As we made our way home, people were shaking our hands and waving from their cars. The allied forces had not yet entered the city, and Karl and I were the only Westerners to be seen. We were embarrassed by their outpourings of gratitude; we were the ones who had been most helped by the Kuwaitis, not they by us. But we were just as delighted that we were now all free and were riding on the same wave of euphoria. We felt that strong bonds had been forged between us during the occupation and that anything that had separated us before it was now forgotten.

We returned to Aziz's house and immediately decided to go in search of souvenirs. There was no shortage of buildings in the area that had been occupied by the Iraqis. In the first one I reeled back with revulsion. The stench was indescribable. Rotting food, human excrement, and the stale smell of body odour and dirty linen were everywhere. The sight was as revolting as the smell. Furniture, pictures and ornaments had been smashed. Books and papers ripped and flung everywhere. Letters and broken crockery were strewn all over the place. The souvenirs we were looking for were all heaped together: there were helmets, live ammunition, military documents, uniforms, gun holsters, kitbags and water canteens. We picked up our booty and carried it into Aziz's garden. We had joined the ranks of the looters.

For all the destruction and brutality and suffering, liberated Kuwait had never looked more beautiful. And the best was yet to come, I thought. I imagined the joy of seeing the allies march in, the Kuwaitis returning, and all the forces of liberation converging in triumph. I foresaw a future better than it had ever been in the past. In the meantime, there was still no electricity and we went to bed early. Sleep took a long time coming, because outside the revellers were still celebrating. The shooting continued.

XXX

It was still grey outside when I woke early on Wednesday morning, February 27, but my mood was bright. Today, surely, the liberation forces would march triumphantly in, Kuwait's leaders would return in a motorcade and salute the cheering crowds. Trucks and tanks carrying the liberators, Arabs and Westerners alike, would cruise down the coast road, while the liberated would run up, jump on the tanks, kiss, hug and shake hands. I had waited for this day so long. I was going to fling my arms around the neck of the first allied soldier I saw.

At 7.15 a.m. Aziz and I, armed with umbrellas, took to the streets. We passed the Sheraton, heading towards the Gulf road. The old reconstructed city gate, a rare relic of Kuwait's past, lay in ruins. I saw several army jeeps flying the American flag stop on the Gulf road. I felt like running up to them, but they moved on. We decided not to walk on the beach side of the road because of the threat of mines. In the middle of the dual carriageway on the central reservation there were rolls of barbed wire. This, we were told, was to stop soldiers entrenched on the beach from fleeing from an amphibious landing. Another rumour had it that Iraqi soldiers were not allowed to wear white underwear which they could use to surrender.

The buildings facing the Gulf were in a sorry state. They had been used as Iraqi fortifications and their windows had been smashed and blocked in to allow for gun slits. Gun emplacements were on the rooftops at every street corner. The parliament building had been punctured by shells from tank fire. Once snow white, it was now streaked with grey from the black rain. One of its wings was burnt black. In front of it was an abandoned Iraqi tank; a big toy bunny-rabbit hung from its turret and an assortment of belongings was scattered on the ground. The red Kuwait Museum was still standing but its walls had been blackened by fire and it had been looted. A dhow — a traditional wooden Arab boat — which had stood in the museum's yard was gone.

A Kuwaiti flag was flying on the Seif Palace. The Amir's mud-coloured working palace had been under reconstruction at the time of the invasion. I knew who had put up the flag — Talal's brother. He had spoken proudly of it the day before. Across from the palace, the state mosque had a newly inscribed plaque. It said it was the mosque of 'Saddam Hussein the Great'.

The skies again darkened and the rain came down. The sea was gun-metal grey and somewhere over the horizon the guns were firing. There were a few cars in the street. Kuwaiti motorists stopped and asked us if we needed a lift. Mistaking Aziz, who wore a tracksuit, for a foreigner, they addressed him in English and he thanked them politely. We began to walk on the beach side of the road and, picking our way carefully, went close to some of the bunkers. They all seemed to have telephones and there were wires all over the beach. There were pots of what looked like half-cooked food and rounds of ammunition. In one bunker there were pin-ups on the wall. In another, two thick books in Arabic, the Koran and the Hadiths, the sayings of the Prophet. Helmets, water canteens, pieces of uniform, bullets and what looked like mini-rockets were scattered all over the beach.

There were no allied soldiers to be seen. Then, as we approached the twin Kuwait Towers, we saw a small group of people in uniform and a few army jeeps on the beach. I also spotted a satellite dish. They must be journalists, I told Aziz, and we began walking faster. It was the CBS reporter Bob McKeown and his camera crew, who I had learned from a BBC report had entered the city ahead of the troops the night before. They were surrounded by a group of jubilant Kuwaitis who were eager to shake hands with the Americans. I was surprised to see Talal there, engaged in conversation with McKeown. When he saw me his eyes widened. He had just been telling the American, who was eager to meet some Westerners, about Karl and me. McKeown called his cameraman and in no time we had done the interview. While we were talking, his attention would drift away. I would notice this later with other journalists. They were all eager to talk, but while you talked, they seemed to be resting, their minds on something else. Of course the fact that they were exhausted had to be borne in mind. Some had driven through the desert, avoiding mine-fields, to get to the city as fast as they could. When they slept, it was only in short naps in the jeep. When they arrived in Kuwait, they fanned out like an army following several leads at the same time. In their uniforms and khaki jeeps, the journalists were the stars in those first few days before the troops arrived in the city.

In return for the CBS interview I was allowed to make an overseas telephone call. It was 9.30 a.m. and I thought I could still catch my sister at her home in Turin. As I listened to the phone ring, I thought I would burst with excitement. Everything was happening so fast I could hardly take it in, let alone savour it. When she heard my voice she cried out with joy and we had one of our most incoherent conversations ever. I think I said very little. She understood I was well, and I was relieved that all my family were well too. I had been worried that my father, who has a heart ailment, might find the anxiety too much for him and fall seriously ill.

While we were still on the beach by the Kuwait Towers a jeep pulled up with a British journalist in it. I walked up and asked him whether he knew anyone from the *Sunday Times*. 'I am from the *Sunday Times*,' he said. It was their diplomatic correspondent Ian Glover-James. As we stood chatting we were joined by Dr Jawad Behbehani, Aziz's friend, whom I had met back in October. On hearing that journalists were looking for evidence of Iraqi atrocities, he suggested we go to the Mubarak Hospital morgue.

In the hospital we had a brief encounter with Kuwaiti bureaucracy. The doctor in charge said he had had no permission from the health authorities to let us view the bodies and also needed the approval of the families of the dead. In fact, the dead Kuwaitis had not been identified and no one knew who their families were. Eventually, we descended to the morgue. I had never seen a dead body before. Dr Sameer Assad, who accompanied us, lifted the sheet from the body of an Iraqi soldier. He was in uniform and looked as if he had died in his sleep. Not so the Kuwaitis. Ian, notebook in hand, went close to examine the wounds. I stood at a distance of 3 metres and only looked furtively at the bodies. Even so, I saw heads split open, broken legs, empty eye sockets. Dr Assad pulled out another corpse. It was wrapped in a cloth stained with dried blood and looked very short. When he uncovered the body I saw there was very little left of the lower half. It had been burned to the bone. Dr Assad said the man had also been shot through the ear and slashed across the throat. But at least he was recognisable, his family would be able to identify him, he said. There was another body in an adjoining room. It too did not seem to be that of a normal size man. When Dr Assad lifted the sheet I could see why. All his limbs, now hardly recognisable, had been broken, his head split and his intestines were hanging out of his slashed stomach. I turned my head away while Dr Assad drew our attention to the burn marks on the man's body. It was a hideous sight. Dr Assad told us that according to hospital records, 465 civilians had been killed since the invasion.

On the way back to Shuwaikh we weaved through trucks and tanks carrying Saudi troops into the city. There were groups of Kuwaitis at every intersection carrying banners welcoming allied troops. Some women gave the Arab warbling wail as we passed.

'This is a historic moment for Kuwait,' Ian said. Indeed it is, I thought, but why doesn't it feel like it? Where is the Amir, the Prime Minister, the commanders? Where are the troops? Where are the bands playing the national anthem? Where is the parade, the pomp, flags and crowds that should go with victory and celebration? The historic moment had somehow shattered into split-seconds of joy, a wave of a hand, a kiss blown to a truckful of Saudi soldiers. It came in fits and starts at the intersections, where small crowds gave way to long stretches of highway empty of revellers.

It was liberation day, but I could no longer rejoice. I had run out of emotional energy. Nothing, I decided, would ever be as exciting as the times when I had pictured the day of liberation in my mind. I had anticipated it so many times over the months, now it was anticlimactic. Reality had taken over from my fantasy.

XXXI

On Thursday afternoon, February 28, I witnessed a military operation carried out with a precision which brought a lump to my throat. I was with Ian Glover-James and my American friend Karl near the British Embassy when I heard the roar of helicopters flying in from the sea. We stopped and looked up. The clouds were pressing down, blotting out the sun, and it looked as if a storm was gathering. The helicopters were making a tremendous noise as they came into sight. Passersby stopped and looked up, and a crowd grew on a piece of wasteland in front of the embassy. Cars stopped in their tracks and drivers got out to watch as one of the helicopters hovered over a ten-storey block of flats overlooking the embassy. A rope came down, quickly followed by a dozen soldiers dressed for combat who were lowered on to the roof. More men dropped from a second helicopter and took up positions on the roof. Two other helicopters approached from the Gulf. One dropped more troops on to the roof of the embassy's commercial building, and the other on to the chancery. In front of the embassy the trees bent violently in the wind of the rotary blades and a cloud of dust gathered as the helicopters climbed sharply and looped away to be replaced by two more. We all stood mesmerised. The British were recapturing the territory in style. At this moment I felt immensely proud to be British. Karl and Ian dismissed it as 'only a show', but what a show!

There was little chance of the Royal Marines encountering any Iraqi stragglers. They had never entered the embassy compound, even after the ambassador left in December.

Three days had passed now since the Iraqis fled and I was looking eagerly for some further manifestation of victory. The only signs were the Kuwaitis who drove in convoys of cars through the streets, sounding their horns and firing their rifles into the air. The Marines had given us only a sniff of the extravaganza we felt we were owed.

The British ambassador arrived that same evening in a similarly staged event. He later told me he too had been overcome by emotion on his arrival. He was less impressed by the methods adopted by the Marines once they hit the ground. They stormed the embassy buildings and turned everything upside down in the chancery. They even opened fire on the bullet-proof glass of the reception area. I later saw the damage.

The next day Karl and I watched the new American ambassador arrive at the US Embassy, also by helicopter, in an equally moving, though less dramatic, ceremony. A large crowd gathered, and US Marines surrounding the embassy signed autographs and posed for pictures holding Kuwaiti babies in their arms. When the helicopters came we waved excitedly, but it all happened too quickly. They disappeared below the embassy walls, discharging the ambassador and his retinue before flying away, leaving us with the grit of their dust in our mouths.

A week later, the British Prime Minister, John Major, paid a brief visit to the embassy and gave our morale a tremendous boost. About thirty of us who had stayed on were invited to meet him, though it was no more than a quick handshake and a few words. He apologised for being delayed by bad weather. We were glad he had come at all. We were grateful for the speed and efficiency with which the embassy had seen to our needs, and the British were among the very few in Kuwait at the time to have somewhere to turn to for help.

In the days after the Iraqi withdrawal, our initial euphoria quickly wore off. Suddenly, nothing seemed very different from before. It was not just the absence of parades and pageantry. Our food was running low and none seemed to be coming in. Bread from Saudi Arabia was held up at the border, and when it arrived four days later, it was stale as old boots. Ian Glover-James and I flagged down a Saudi army truck and asked for some of the bread it was carrying to the troops. The Saudis stopped and gave us a few bags of Arab flat bread and were immediately beseiged by crowds of Kuwaiti children, their hands outstretched. With no electricity, at night we sat in unheated rooms around kerosene lamps and candle-light. The streets were black as pitch. Water was also in short supply and petrol even harder to find.

I felt a distinct sense of déjà vu when two Syrian soldiers arrived at our front gate and asked for water. Then I was stopped at a checkpoint in Salwa where a Kuwaiti soldier asked not for my documents, but for food. The gunshots into the sky were constant and reports of injuries from the celebratory gunfire began coming in. Some people also received wounds from mines left behind by the Iraqis. Soon, everyone seemed to be carrying arms, including teenagers, and, before the allied forces arrived, civilians were manning roadblocks, checking our papers. Only four days from when the Iraqis had fled, did the first Kuwaiti troops take over the checkpoints. They couldn't have been more courteous when I showed them my British passport. 'Ala rasi,' they said, a mark of respect to someone to whom they feel a debt of honour.

As time went by, the mood changed. I saw Arab civilians being dragged from their cars, their hands held high. Others were made to crouch against walls while they were searched, before being taken away to who knows where. The main targets were the Palestinians. They were, as ever, in the middle of a sandwich. For more than forty years they had been a political football in their search for a homeland, and now found themselves again the losers. Many had only themselves to blame. They had jumped on the Saddam bandwagon in the early days of the occupation to take revenge against their former employers and the regime that had given them a temporary home, but no true identity through citizenship. But there were others who were utterly loyal to their adoptive state throughout the war. In fact the Palestinian reaction to the war was remarkably diverse. Some openly sided with Iraq and betrayed and looted. Some joined the Popular Army set up by the Iraqis soon after the invasion to establish quick control of the country. Some even manned checkpoints in the early days, and when the air war began, PLO commandos moved into the Palestinian district of Hawalli, ostensibly to maintain order but also to dig in in preparation for the ground offensive.

Other Palestinians were among the most helpful and kindly people in the whole population, especially to those of us in hiding. They brought food, and screened us from Iraqi visits at great risk to themselves. Some joined the resistance movement and several among those who were captured were executed.

Palestinian resistance fighters were said to have been responsible for the assassination of Khodar Mubarak, the former Kuwaiti chief of military police, who was top of the Kuwaiti resistance movement's hit list as a traitor. In spite of this, after liberation, many Kuwaitis seemed to view all Palestinians as active collaborators, and fear of post-war reprisals drove more than half the 400,000 Palestinians living in Kuwait to flee the country.

Many Kuwaitis were appalled at the summary justice meted out to Palestinians. They were being seized on the streets and detained and tortured. Known collaborators were executed. Some sympathetic Kuwaitis went to detention points to secure their release. In Salwa, I saw two Kuwaiti civilians take away Mushtaq's sister who shared a flat in Vladimir's building. Mushtaq managed to escape and his sister was later released. But by this time she was too afraid to talk of her experiences.

There was no law or order; it was like a cowboy town with rifles being fired constantly and groups of outlaws running amok. The Kuwaiti government was coming back in dribs and drabs and when they finally assembled, they immediately clamped a state of martial law on the country. It did little to halt the lawlessness. The government's failure to restore order and provide adequate food supplies and services angered many Kuwaitis. They had to wait ten days after liberation before any food and water came in. Those citizens who had stayed on during the occupation received no recognition, nor were they involved in efforts to restore normal life. The government was reluctant to use the local Co-operatives for food distribution, even though they had done a splendid job during the occupation. It apparently had no confidence in those who ran the Co-ops under Iraqi supervision. Disillusionment over the government's handling of the situation was so deeply felt that one Kuwaiti told me: 'We'd rather be a British colony than go back to the system we had before.'

On February 28 there was a sign of the shape of things to come. A prominent Kuwaiti lawyer and a former deputy, Hamed Al Joa'an, was a victim of an assassination attempt. He had been responsible for the removal of a member of the ruling family from the government for his role in the 1982 stock market crash. Ian Glover-James and I went to see Al Joa'an in the hospital where he was guarded by armed civilians. He told us a Kuwaiti had shot him, though he could not identify him. He had foreseen an attempt on his life. In November there were reports that some younger members of the ruling family were planning to set up private militias, ostensibly to deal with collaborators, but also to tackle opponents of the regime. There was also talk about a close relative of the Amir going to Syria to recruit 3,000 Syrians for one such militia, while a group of Interior Ministry agents slipped into Kuwait during the occupation to recruit men for a pro-Al Sabah underground movement. In London, Scotland Yard was said to have offered protection to a leading opposition member, Dr Ahmed Khatib, after a threat to his life.

All this reinforced the belief among activists that the ruling family would not relinquish any power once it returned to Kuwait. They set about producing a document demanding the reinstatement of parliament and the formation of a 'competent people's government'. This would bar the ruling family from key cabinet positions and demand the naming of names of those responsible for the bungle which left the country defenceless when Iraq invaded. The document was supported by all opposition groups, including religious factions. Statements by the Prime Minister on his return to Kuwait that a democratic system would be installed once the country was back on its feet did nothing to appease the opposition. They turned for protection and support to the British and Americans, who had brought back the ruling family but who had made clear to them they expected democratic rule in the future.

Aziz and I told the British ambassador, Michael Weston, of the assassination attempt while Aziz sought protection for other politicians. He promised to inform the Foreign Office of the incident and met other opposition leaders to hear their views. We then went to the American Embassy and saw one of the ambassador's aides. A day or two later the American ambassador visited Hamed Al Joa'an in hospital and offered American doctors to treat him.

But if some Kuwaitis were afraid for their safety, they were also defiant. They seized the opportunity of the huge press contingent to voice their dissatisfaction with the government, while, at the same time, the government was speaking in much the same terms as it had been before the crisis. There was a chasm between those who had stayed on and those who had left. I, naturally, having shared the experiences of the occupation, shared the Kuwaiti people's disappointment. The country was in disarray and I saw no quick solution or return to normality.

It was about this time that I learned of the death of three dear friends. Zeinab and Kahtan, with whom I had shared so much in the early days of the occupation, were killed by allied bombs while they watched from their garden the withdrawal of Iraqi troops on the last night of the war. This was devastating news. It had hardly sunk in when I was told that Jerzy, my Polish architect friend, had been killed in a car crash while on his way to Ahmedi three days later. I was deeply distressed.

The drain and strain of the past seven months were finally taking their toll. The liberation had been a letdown and my post-liberation hopes were coming to nothing. For the first time it was I who needed to escape.

I asked the British ambassador to help me to leave. He quickly fixed me up with an RAF flight to Riyadh. On March 10 I boarded a Hercules transport and took off from Kuwait Airport. It was close to ruins. It had been the scene of one of the last battles between the US Marines and the retreating Iraqi forces. As we took off, I saw for the first time dozens of oil wells burning, the flames and smoke rising high into the sky and casting a dark pall over desert and city alike. The clouds seemed endless. It all seemed a fitting symbol of the plight of the country I was leaving behind.

Epilogue

Counting the costs and gains of an experience like the Iraqi occupation of Kuwait is an intricate and painful process. In material terms, I lost my home and many of my possessions. I also lost my job. But my losses went beyond those. I lost three friends, and in a way I lost Clem too. In sharing the early, most dramatic moments of the invasion, it put our relationship under a microscope and we could both see the hairline cracks of before widen into deeper ones. I think I also lost some of my innocence.

But whatever the losses, they pale beside those of the Kuwaitis. They bore the brunt of the Iraqi brutality and thousands died as a result. Hardly a family has been left untouched. I could do little more than grieve with them. As never before in my five years in Kuwait, I felt as at one with them as an outsider could. Vladimir Dimitrijevic once said during the height of the occupation: 'We were with them when the going was good, we should be with them when it is bad.' The fact that I was, was my greatest gain.

War is suffering in its most concentrated form and yet the very hardship, brutality and fear can bring out the best in us. I was not prepared for the contradictions that became apparent the longer I stayed. When I first saw people managing to enjoy themselves during the occupation I found it hard to reconcile it with the events taking place only a few hundred metres from their barbecue parties. Yet soon I too had moments of enjoying myself and only then realised that it was all part of easing the stress of our lives. It is impossible to weep for six months non-stop. It seemed just as incongruous to sit in the garden at dusk with the sound of shells and bombs exploding and watch the sun go down as if everything were normal. Yet sunsets were there to be enjoyed more than ever. Nothing makes life feel more precious than a threat to it, just as nothing makes you fight harder to survive than a scent of danger.

I counted even my arrest and release as accomplishments, as gains in experience and survival. As the months went by my life became full of such little and large triumphs. In some ways life under occupation was simple, black and white. The good and the bad, the right and the wrong, seemed clear enough and I had no doubt that I was on the right side. Kuwait had been wronged and Saddam Hussein was the wrong-doer.

I could not cry over the Iraqi dead, as some outside did, while the people of Kuwait were being brutalised daily. But nothing is so black and white as to remove dilemmas. I struggled daily to make right decisions and judgements which could have meant the difference between safety and capture, even life and death. I wrestled constantly over who to trust, whether my intended good deeds would endanger my friends. I had to judge which roads were safe, where the roadblocks might be today and whether to keep gathering information and risk writing letters. I had to decide when to move house and where to move to or whether to stay where I was. There were also moral dilemmas. When I rummaged through people's homes and belongings to steal what would be useful to others in hiding, I told myself it was necessary. But if the Iraqis also stole out of need, was I any less of a thief? Some Britons sought freedom by acquiring Irish travel documents. Others rejected the idea of resorting to such a device. Ski would have nothing to do with a suggestion that he might get a Polish passport by virtue of his Polish origins. I used my Yugoslav passport and justified it as a way to stay in Kuwait, not leave.

There were divisions among us over the ethics of those from outside who came to Baghdad to plead for the release of hostages. Some, including me, called them grovellers and thought they were reinforcing the hand of Saddam Hussein. Yet while deploring their efforts, I was only too happy to hope that Mohammed Ali would help to get Clem released. Eoin MacDougald refused to sign the petition by other Canadians in Kuwait pleading with Saddam for their own release. The tone of the letter, he said, was enough to turn his stomach. Such ethical conflicts tended to make us look at ourselves more closely. My initial reason for staying on in Kuwait was simply that it had been my home for five years and all I had was there. I had no husband and children, although of course there was Clem. I also felt I had a professional duty to stay to try to report on events from inside. Later, that grew to a moral one as well when I began to feel a close solidarity with the Kuwaitis and an affinity with Kuwait itself.

There were risks attached and risk-taking can be addictive. But I did try to calculate my risks carefully and this was probably why I escaped unscathed. When Alan wrote in December, a few days after all the hostages were freed, he tried to shake me into an awareness of the danger I faced if I stayed. He was also afraid I might get hooked on danger. I knew this was a possibility. The occupation for me was by no means without its thrills. There were a number of occasions when I felt the adrenalin pumping as a result of that odd mixture of fear and excitement. But they seemed to be the inevitable reactions of someone of my temperament in my kind of job and as such inseparable. I regarded these as part of the profit and loss account.

What should have been a gain was the Kuwaitis' need to win the peace as they and their allies had won the war. In their plight they seemed to have a unique opportunity to shake off the stereotyped image of Arabs as untrustworthy, devious and bloodthirsty. That they failed to grab the chance was not the fault of those who stayed behind. Throughout the occupation most Kuwaitis rejected the idea of taking any indiscriminate retribution against those among them, especially the Palestinians, who may have collaborated with the Iraqis. Others, however, took the law into their own hands with a brutality as savage as Saddam's own. This and the prolonged agony of the Kurds in the aftermath of the war gave it all a distressing finale. But this is the reality of wars. They end with few winners and Kuwait's was a victory of pyrrhic proportions. I shared its anguish; I now mourn in its misery.

Jadranka Porter was born in Yugoslavia and educated at the University of Belgrade. She later studied in Sri Lanka. After living in Iraq and Bahrain, she moved to Kuwait in 1985 to work as a journalist for the *Arab Times*.